EDYTHE MAE GORDON

SELECTED WORKS OF EDYTHE MAE GORDON

AFRICAN-AMERICAN WOMEN WRITERS, 1910–1940

HENRY LOUIS GATES, JR. *GENERAL EDITOR*

Jennifer Burton *Associate Editor*

OTHER TITLES IN THIS SERIES

EDYTHE MAE GORDON

SELECTED WORKS OF
EDYTHE MAE GORDON

Introduction by
LORRAINE ELENA ROSES

G. K. HALL & CO.
An Imprint of Simon & Schuster Macmillan
New York

Prentice Hall International
London Mexico City New Delhi Singapore Sydney Toronto

G. K. Hall & Co.
An Imprint of Simon & Schuster Macmillan
1633 Broadway
New York, NY 10019

Library of Congress Catalog Card Number: 96-5811

Printed in the United States of America

Printing Number
1 2 3 4 5 6 7 8 9 10

Library of Congress Cataloging-in-Publication Data

Gordon, Edythe Mae, b. 1896.
    [Selections]
    Selected works of Edythe Mae Gordon / Edythe Mae Gordon ;
introduction by Lorraine Elena Roses.
        p.   cm.—(African American women writers, 1910–1940)
    Includes bibliographical references (p.   ).
    ISBN 0-7838-1420-8 (alk. paper)
    1. Afro-American women—Literary collections.   2. Afro-Americans—
Literary collections.   3. Roses, Lorraine Elena, 1943–
I. Title   II. Series.
PS3513.0579A6   1996
818'.5209—dc20   96-5811
                                                                        CIP

This paper meets the requirements of ANSI/NISO Z39.48.1992 (Permanence of Paper).

C O N T E N T S

CONTENTS

Contents

GENERAL EDITORS' PREFACE

The past decade of our literary history might be thought of as the era of African-American women writers. Culminating in the awarding of the Pulitzer Prize to Toni Morrison and Rita Dove and the Nobel Prize for Literature to Toni Morrison in 1993 and characterized by the presence of several writers—Toni Morrison, Alice Walker, Maya Angelou, and the Delaney Sisters, among others—on the *New York Times* Best Seller List, the shape of the most recent period in our literary history has been determined in large part by the writings of black women.

This, of course, has not always been the case. African-American women authors have been publishing their thoughts and feelings at least since 1773, when Phillis Wheatley published her book of poems in London, thereby bringing poetry directly to bear upon the philosophical discourse over the African's "place in nature" and his or her place in the great chain of being. The scores of words published by black women in America in the nineteenth century—most of which were published in extremely limited editions and never reprinted—have been republished in new critical editions in the forty-volume *Schomburg Library of Nineteenth-Century Black Women Writers*. The critical response to that series has led to requests from scholars and students alike for a similar series, one geared to the work by black women published between 1910 and the beginning of World War Two.

African-American Women Writers, 1910–1940 is designed to bring back into print many writers who otherwise would be unknown to contemporary readers, and to increase the availability of lesser-known texts by established writers who originally published during this critical period in African-American letters. This series implicitly acts as a chronological sequel to the Schomburg series, which focused on the origins of the black female literary tradition in America.

In less than a decade, the study of African-American women's writings has grown from its promising beginnings into a firmly established field in departments of English, American Studies, and African-American Studies. A comparison of the form and function of the original series and this sequel illustrates this dramatic shift. The *Schomburg Library* was published at the cusp of focused academic investigation into the interplay between race and gender. It covered the extensive period from the publication of Phillis Wheatley's *Poems on Various Subjects, Religious and Moral* in 1773 through the "Black Women's Era" of 1890–1910, and was designed to be an inclusive series of the major early texts by black women writers. The Schomburg Library provided a historical backdrop for black women's writings of the 1970s and 1980s, including the works of writers such as Toni Morrison, Alice Walker, Maya Angelou, and Rita Dove.

African-American Women Writers, 1910–1940 continues our effort to provide a new generation of readers access to texts—historical, sociological, and literary—that have been largely "unread" for most of this century. The series bypasses works that are important both to the period and the tradition, but that are readily available, such as Zora Neale Hurston's *Their Eyes Were Watching God*, Jessie Fauset's *Plum Bun* and *There Is Confusion*, and Nella Larsen's *Quicksand* and *Passing*. Our goal is to provide access to a wide variety of rare texts. The series includes Fauset's two other novels, *The Chinaberry Tree: A Novel of American Life* and *Comedy: American Style*, and Hurston's short play *Color Struck*, since these are not yet widely available. It also features works by virtually unknown writers, such as *A Tiny Spark*, Christina Moody's slim volume of poetry self-published in 1910, and *Reminiscences of School Life, and Hints on Teaching*, written by Fanny Jackson Coppin in the last year of her life (1913), a multi-genre work combining an autobiographical sketch and reflections on trips to England and South Africa, complete with pedagogical advice.

Cultural studies' investment in diverse resources allows the historic scope of the *African-American Women Writers* series to be more focused than the *Schomburg Library* series, which covered works written over a 137-year period. With few exceptions, the authors included in the *African-American Women Writers* series wrote their major works between 1910 and 1940. The texts reprinted include all the works by each particular author that are not otherwise readily obtainable. As a result, two volumes contain works originally published after 1940. The Charlotte Hawkins Brown volume includes her book of etiquette published in 1941, *The Correct Thing To Do—To Say—To Wear*. One of the poetry volumes contains Maggie Pogue Johnson's *Fallen Blossoms*, published in 1951, a compilation of all her previously published and unpublished poems.

Excavational work by scholars during the past decade has been crucial to the development of *African-American Women Writers, 1910–1940*. Germinal bibliographical sources such as Ann Allen Shockley's *Afro-American Women Writers 1746–1933* and Maryemma Graham's *Database of African-American Women Writers* made the initial identification of texts possible. Other works were brought to our attention by scholars who wrote letters sharing their research. Additional texts by selected authors were then added, so that many volumes contain the complete oeuvres of particular writers. Pieces by authors without enough published work to fill an entire volume were grouped with other pieces by genre.

The two types of collections, those organized by author and those organized by genre, bring out different characteristics of black women's writings of the period. The collected works of the literary writers illustrate that many of them were experimenting with a variety of forms. Mercedes Gilbert's volume, for example, contains her 1931 collection *Selected Gems of Poetry, Comedy, and Drama, Etc.*, as well as her 1938 novel *Aunt Sarah's Wooden God*. Georgia Douglas Johnson's volume contains her plays and short stories in addition to her poetry. Sarah Lee Brown Fleming's volume combines her 1918 novel *Hope's Highway* with her 1920 collection of poetry, *Clouds and Sunshine*.

The generic volumes both bring out the formal and thematic similarities among many of the writings and highlight the striking individuality of particular writers. Most of the plays in the volume of one-acts are social dramas whose tragic endings can be clearly attributed to miscegenation and racism. Within the context of these other plays, Marita Bonner's surrealistic theatrical vision becomes all the more striking.

The volumes of *African-American Women Writers, 1910–1940* contain reproductions of more than one hundred previously published texts, including twenty-nine plays, seventeen poetry collections, twelve novels, six autobiographies, five collections of short biographical sketches, three biographies, three histories of organizations, three black histories, two anthologies, two sociological studies, a diary, and a book of etiquette. Each volume features an introduction by a contemporary scholar that provides crucial biographical data on each author and the historical and critical context of her work. In some cases, little information on the authors was available outside of the fragments of biographical data contained in the original introduction or in the text itself. In these instances, editors have documented the libraries and research centers where they tried to find information, in the hope that subsequent scholars will continue the necessary search to find the "lost" clues to the women's stories in the rich stores of papers, letters, photographs, and other primary materials scattered throughout the country that have yet to be fully catalogued.

Many of the thrilling moments that occurred during the development of this series were the result of previously fragmented pieces of these women's histories suddenly coming together, such as Adele Alexander's uncovering of an old family photograph picturing her own aunt with Addie Hunton, the author Alexander was researching. Claudia Tate's examination of Georgia Douglas Johnson's papers in the Moorland-Spingarn Research Center of Howard University resulted in the discovery of a wealth of previously unpublished work.

The slippery quality of race itself emerged during the construction of the series. One of the short novels originally intended for inclusion in the series had to be cut when the family of the author protested that the writer was not of African descent. Another case involved Louise Kennedy's sociological study *The Negro Peasant Turns Inward*. The fact that none of the available biographical material on Kennedy specifically mentioned race, combined with some coded criticism in a review in the *Crisis*, convinced editor Sheila Smith McKoy that Kennedy was probably white.

These women, taken together, began to chart the true vitality, and complexity, of the literary tradition that African-American women have generated, using a wide variety of forms. They testify to the fact that the monumental works of Hurston, Larsen, and Fauset, for example, emerged out of a larger cultural context; they were not exceptions or aberrations. Indeed, their contributions to American literature and culture, as this series makes clear, were fundamental not only to the shaping of the African-American tradition but to the American tradition as well.

Henry Louis Gates, Jr.
Jennifer Burton

PUBLISHER'S NOTE

In the *African-American Women Writers, 1910–1940* series, G. K. Hall not only is making available previously neglected works that in many cases have been long out of print, we are also, whenever possible, publishing these works in facsimiles reprinted from their original editions including, when available, reproductions of original title pages, copyright pages, and photographs.

When it was not possible for us to reproduce a complete facsimile edition of a particular work (for example, if the original exists only as a handwritten draft or is too fragile to be reproduced), we have attempted to preserve the essence of the original by resetting the work exactly as it originally appeared. Therefore, any typographical errors, strikeouts, or other anomalies reflect our efforts to give the reader a true sense of the original work.

We trust that these facsimile and reprint editions, together with the new introductory essays, will be both useful and historically enlightening to scholars and students alike.

INTRODUCTION

BY LORRAINE ELENA ROSES

When I am cold and buried deep away,
And have no zest to live or to return,
Come to my grave and flower-strew the clay,
And dance and sing, but never weep or mourn.

Edythe Mae Gordon, "Buried Deep"

In her last extant piece of writing (1938),[1] Edythe Mae Gordon invites her readers to pay a visit to her grave and joyfully adorn it with flowers. Sadly, we cannot do so because she vanished, leaving no monument other than a small body of writing.

Edythe Mae Gordon made her first public appearance as a writer in 1928, in the debut issue of the *Saturday Evening Quill*, a little magazine edited by her husband, Eugene, and published in Boston. The *Quill* was founded in the heyday of the Harlem, or New Negro, Renaissance by a group of black Bostonians; it is an important, and still unexplored, source for the study of black intellectual and literary life in Boston during the late 1920s. Half the founders were women, including Helene Johnson (b. 1906), Gertrude Parthenia McBrown (1902–1989), and short story writer, later novelist Dorothy West[2] (b. 1907)—the only Quill club member who has remained in the public eye.

The short story "Subversion" in the *Quill*'s first annual issue (1928) is accompanied by a biographical note that furnishes us with some of the few clues we possess about Edythe Mae Gordon's life and career:

Edythe Mae Gordon was born in Washington, D.C. and educated in the public schools there and in special courses at Boston and Harvard Universities. "Subversion" is her first published story. She is the wife of Eugene Gordon.

The second annual issue of the *Quill* (1929) carried another story by Edythe Mae Gordon, entitled "If Wishes Were Horses," along with six of her poems. The biographical note in this issue informs us that "Subversion" had been listed by the O. Henry Memorial Award Prize Committee as one of the distinguished "short short stories" of 1928—an honor indeed if we recall that writing by black authors was routinely ignored by the white publishing establishment of the time. This note does not identify her as "the wife of Eugene Gordon" but as "secretary" of the Saturday Evening Quill Club.

The 1930 issue, with which the *Quill* ceased publication, carried five more poems and a third story ("Hostess") by Gordon. The biographical note supplies another nugget of information, namely, that Gordon had contributed earlier poems to *Opportunity: A Journal of Negro Life*. [3]

These not very revealing notes are the only published evidence about Edythe Mae Gordon from her day. All state that she took courses at Boston University, and university records support this claim. Her birth date is listed as June 4, 1900, on one university document and June 4, 1898, on another, but Census records for 1900 indicate she was born in June of 1896. [4] The discrepancy could mean that Gordon felt self-conscious about being older than most college students and decided to erase some years from her age. [5] Boston University records show that her secondary school preparation was at the "M Street School" in Washington, DC, from 1912 to 1916, which is consistent with the *Quill* note. [6] The M Street School, a black high school, was well known in educational circles because almost all of its graduates went on to higher education at a time when most American students of any color did not do so. It was also famous for its distinguished faculty, which included, among a long list of outstanding educators, Ann Julia Cooper and Carter Woodson. [7] Edythe Mae Gordon might have studied with poet and novelist Jessie Fauset, who taught French at the school from 1906 to 1920, but she probably graduated too early to study with Angelina Weld Grimké (1880–1958), who joined the faculty in 1916. Edythe Mae Gordon entered Boston University as a part-time student taking "special courses" in 1926, and continued her studies there for nine academic years. She was a full-time undergraduate from 1931 to 1934, earning a bachelor of science degree in Religious Education and Social Services on June 11, 1934. Another year of full-time study brought her a master's degree from the School of Social Services, later the School of Social Work, on July 10, 1935, at a time when stiff racial and gender barriers prevented many African-American women from pursuing graduate study at white universities. She was thirty-nine years old.

There is no evidence that Gordon held any jobs during her years at Boston University, although most students at that time (especially those in the social services program) did work their way through school. Perhaps the Gordons simply decided they could manage on Eugene's income as a staff writer for the *Boston Post*, a daily newspaper.

Edythe Mae Gordon's master's thesis was entitled "The Status of the Negro Woman in the United States from 1619 to 1865." It contains none of the acknowledgments indicating a special relationship with faculty members or others who are often seen in such documents, but university records indicate that Gordon's major advisor was Professor Albert Morris, presumably not an African American, who lived in suburban Needham.[8]

In the absence of any testimony from Edythe Mae Gordon or her peers, it is difficult to speculate about the quality of her experience at Boston University or about her relationships with other students. Her name does not appear in the various student organizations included in *Tophos*, the school yearbook—perhaps her role as Eugene Gordon's wife required that she assist him and manage their household when not occupied with her studies—although the 1934 edition has a small photograph of Gordon as one of fourteen graduates (apparently the only African American) in the School of Religious Education program (10). She is not on the roster of members of the alumni association, nor does any news of her appear in the alumni magazine, *Bostonia*.[9] The photograph on p. 2 shows Gordon's hair combed into a cap, flapper style, framing her oval face. In contrast to the hard-eyed heroines she described in her short stories, she smiles sweetly, perhaps a bit shyly, for the camera. She is wearing a scoop-necked blouse with crocheted edges and a chain punctuated with pearls.

Gordon and her husband evidently moved fairly often. Cambridge voter registration records for 1920 show the Gordons living at 66 Inman Street in that city.[10] Boston University directory records show five different addresses for Edythe Mae Gordon: 21 Outlook Road and 37 Oakley Street, both in Dorchester, in 1931; 32 Copley Street, Cambridge (the address given for the editorial offices of the *Quill* some years earlier), in 1928 and 1929. In 1933 the records show a move across the river to 198 Chambers Street, Boston, and then again, to 19 Braddock Park, in the city's South End. It is difficult to say whether these changes signify simply a search for more reasonable rents or changes in the Gordons' lives, but evidence from the Boston city directories[11] suggests all was not well by 1932; in that year the directory gives separate addresses for Edythe Mae Gordon and Eugene F. Gordon: 19 Braddock Park for her and 198 Chambers Street for him (as well as a business listing at the *Boston Post* building, 259 Washington Street). This information continues to appear through 1935, strongly suggesting that the Gordons were experiencing marital strife. The 1936 directory shows no change in Eugene Gordon's address, but Edythe Mae Gordon has moved to 156 Warren Avenue, very close to Braddock Park, in a block that included a towel and apron supply company, two tailors, a Chinese laundry, and the Advent Christian Church and Publication Society in the buildings adjacent to and across from hers. In 1938 Edythe Mae Gordon reappears at 198 Chambers Street, but Eugene's name does not appear in that or any later city directories.

No occupation is given for Edythe in the city directories until 1935, when she is identified as a "student," but in 1937 and 1938 she appears as an "author," publicly assuming an identity centered on her writing. In 1939 no listing appears for Edythe Mae Gordon in the city directory, but records held at the Probate and Family Court reveal that she filed for divorce from Eugene in April of

1942. Afterward she effectively disappears from view. A search of Commonwealth of Massachusetts death records for the years 1936 to 1955 shows no reference to Edythe Mae Gordon, and my efforts to trace her beyond this point have been unsuccessful. Did she remarry and take a new surname? Did she return to her birthplace in Washington, DC? Did she die in her mid-forties or simply stop submitting her work for publication?

Only two additional clues have come to light. In November of 1938 Boston University sent a duplicate transcript for Gordon to "the North Carolina Division of Certification," so she may have left Boston for a social work position in North Carolina. Also in 1938, two new poems, "Sonnet for June" and "Buried Deep," by Edythe Mae Gordon, appeared in *Negro Voices* (13), a collection edited by Beatrice M. Murphy[12] of Washington, DC, who describes Gordon in a note as "the chairman of the Boston Literary Workshop Group which she organized in 1936." I can find no further mention of Gordon anywhere.

Eugene Gordon's writing career is a great deal easier to document, yet he too has been unjustly relegated to near oblivion. Born in 1890 in Oviedo, Florida (ten miles northeast of Orlando in the country around Eatonville and Sanford immortalized by Zora Neale Hurston), he graduated from Howard University in 1917 and subsequently served in the armed forces. In Boston, as of 1919, he wrote for the *Boston Post* while serving as president of the Saturday Evening Quill Club and editor of its magazine. *Who's Who in Colored America* for the years 1938–1940 contains a biographical entry and photograph of Eugene, listing him as a "newspaper man," who married Edythe Mae Chapman on January 10, 1916.[13] This information allows us to deduce that Edythe Mae Gordon's birth name was Chapman.

At the *Boston Post* from 1919 to 1940, Eugene Gordon rose from reporter to editor of short stories and serials to contributor of editorials. His articles also appeared in such mainstream magazines as the *American Mercury, Plain Talk*, and *Scribner's. Who's Who in Colored America* identifies Gordon as a "member of the Communist Party of America" and his articles[14] do indeed reveal him as a stalwart proponent of Marxist principles of class struggle and an advocate of both racial and gender equality. This information, useful to anyone who wishes to study African Americans on the Left, also supplies grounds for conjecture about Edythe Mae Gordon's beliefs but no verification that she shared her husband's ideological convictions.

The year that Edythe Mae Gordon received her master's degree (1935) also saw publication by Eugene Gordon and Cyril Briggs of a pamphlet entitled "The Position of Negro Women."[15] Briggs, a radical activist born in Nevis, British West Indies, was noted for his commitment to black nationalism and to the political program of the Communist (Third) International. He edited *The Crusader*, the official organ of "the African Blood Brotherhood and the Hamitic League of the World."[16] Although the title of the Gordon/Briggs pamphlet resembles that of Edythe's thesis, the two works have little in common. The thesis dwells on the antebellum era of American history, while the pamphlet relies instead on Department of Labor statistics from 1910 to 1930 to document the fact that the majority of African-American women found employment only as domestic servants. Still, it seems likely that there was significant convergence of interest on race and gender issues on the part of both Gordons.

The militancy of the pamphlet contrasts sharply with the stylistic restraint of Edythe's thesis. Briggs and Eugene Gordon argue forcefully for coalition building among white and black workers and for new legislation, and call for strikes as strategies toward the achievement of racial and gender equality. In contrast, Edythe Mae Gordon concludes her thesis rather laconically, asserting that black women must "fight" for equality. She may have supported the actions proposed by her husband, but it is impossible to tell as she does not outline any strategies that will enable black women to escape their double oppression.

Eugene later moved to New York City, where he continued his career as a journalist. He died there in 1974 at age eighty-one, having written at different points in his long career for such vastly different publications as *The National Guardian*, *New Masses* (which he also edited), and *National Geographic*.[17] An obituary in

The Daily World (successor to *The Daily Worker*) makes no mention of Edythe Mae but notes that "his wife, June, well known in labor and Jewish activity, died in 1957."[18] Listed as Eugene's survivors are four brothers—Ernest, Leroy, Theodore, and Fred—a son, Eugene Jr. (presumably by June), and a granddaughter, Chelwie.

Unlike some of her Harlem Renaissance contemporaries, Gordon's creative writing is not overtly concerned with race matters. Instead, it centers on the exploration of personal values and their shaping influence on intimate, especially marital, relationships.

In her first *Quill* story, "Subversion," Edythe Mae Gordon depicts a struggling musician, John Marley, who knows he is dying and yearns to recapture the love and approval of his indifferent wife, Lena. Quite by chance Marley discovers that Lena is having an affair with his friend, the prosperous realtor Charles Delany, and that Delany is the father of the child Marley thought was his. In Marley's view, his marriage depends on how much money he can amass: "He would then have more money . . . Lena would then love him as she had long ago" (16). In characterizing Marley in this way, Gordon seems to be insisting on a fateful confusion between money and love. The story ends with a confrontation in which Marley does not accuse the couple, but insinuates knowledge of their secret, thus leaving them to live with their guilt. The story is told from Marley's perspective and the images are somber, connoting darkness and decline, lending emphasis to Marley's despair.

Themes of betrayal and marital disappointment surface again in the story Edythe Mae Gordon published the following year, "If Wishes Were Horses." (This title recalls the maxim "If wishes were horses, beggars would ride.") The main character, Fred Pomeroy, visits a gypsy in a tent by the beach and is perplexed by her prediction that his wife, Rachel, will soon "be able to realize her desires" and "do some of the things she has long wished to do" (52). Pomeroy, a department store clerk with few prospects for advancement, is mystified by this prediction. With a shift in perspective the story reveals that Rachel does indeed get her wish to sail to Europe—thanks to the $50,000 insurance check she collects upon Pomeroy's sudden death. Gordon attains a new level of complexity in this story, using foreshadowing techniques and delving into her characters' dreams.

In both stories Gordon seems to be exploring the corrosive effects of capitalist values on personal relationships. She may also have been using gender inversion to mask disappointing marital experiences of her own: both Pomeroy and Marley are men whose spouses despise them for their penury and measure their value by the size of their wallets or life insurance policies. Their wives exploit them and remain with them only to keep up appearances; the males, in turn, see themselves as having no worth.

Edythe Mae Gordon's last extant story is "Hostess," published in the 1930 issue of the *Quill*. Here she depicts a black woman starstruck by the glitter of Harlem nightlife. Mazie, described as "thin, pert, yellow," is enticed by Bill, a saxophonist, who is "heavy, brown-skinned, and wearing a gray-checked suit," to go on the road with him. As the story opens, Mazie is at the point of regretting having abandoned a husband who provided her with material comfort for the dubious pleasure of following "a red-hot sheik from Harlem." Finding herself alone, pregnant, and broke, she seizes on the idea that her husband will take her back: "One thing about him, he had always been broadminded. He was the one person in the world who'd understand. She'd tell him of how Bill had deserted her when her money was gone. The yellow dog" (56). The outcome for Mazie is a grim as it was for the male characters in the two previous stories. Discovering that she has been replaced by another woman (in fact, the very friend who advised her not to try her husband's patience), she overdoses on a sleeping potion.

This story may be Gordon's comment on the corrupting influence of dissolute Harlem lifestyles during the 1920s, or it may offer a corollary to the previous two stories, suggesting that African Americans are no different from other Americans suffering from capitalist delusions. Since Gordon's stories do not emphasize race, but rather the corrupting influence of money on personal relationships and family stability, the latter reading offers more coherence.

As for the downbeat endings, it is not be surprising to find Edythe Mae Gordon writing in a pessimistic vein at the onset of the Great Depression, a time when ". . . the fog of despair hung over the land."[19] However, the effects of the stock market crash were felt only after these stories were published.

All three stories, written in the classic short story tradition of O. Henry and de Maupassant, are filled with disillusionment, as if to question the institution of marriage itself, although they may also reflect the author's own unhappy experience in marriage. Probing issues of class rather than of color, they do not fit into the theoretical scheme outlined in Edythe Mae Gordon's master's thesis. Her trenchant depiction of women as unloving and exploitative wives matches those of Dorothy West in such stories as "An Unimportant Man," also published in the *Saturday Evening Quill*. West has indicated that her depictions reflect conflicts between her own parents witnessed in the middle-class home where she was raised. In Edythe's case we have no autobiographical testimony to suggest congruencies or patterns; indeed, the information we do possess points not to middle-class origins but to a working-class home run by women, where men were absent.[20]

The paradoxes of Edythe Mae Gordon's life and writing do not end here, since her poetry is written in yet another voice. Rhythmic, lilting, and permeated with themes of desire, the poems published in the *Saturday Evening Quill* stand in stark contrast to the restraint of the short stories. They are remarkable for their expressed sensuality ("Young Love"), interest in the body ("Tribute"), and insistence that love be proffered on equal terms ("Love Me").

Edythe Mae Gordon's master's thesis displays a third dimension of her production. As an intellectual document, it constitutes a work of incipient theorizing about the intersection of gender and race in America, and specifically among African-American women. Its preface indicates that the author is aware of breaking ground: "It is my intention to set forth the legalistic viewpoint, which gives the theoretical treatment of the Negro woman, and to follow this with material which will show the actual treatment and her status in my analyses" (1). Designed "to examine the legal, social, religious, economic, and educational status of Afro-American women," it was undertaken to "stimulate further study in this neglected field of Negro history" (1). Gordon was apparently interested both in rescuing the history of black women and in exploring the formation of racial and class hierarchies in American society. She was also appropriating an academic occasion to engage in historical writing about race issues before a white audience, that of her professors at Boston University.

Edythe Mae Gordon indicates that she was aware of the new field of "Negro History" by citing Carter G. Woodson's work. She also quotes from Nancy Cunard's anthology, *Negro*, and from Charlotte Hawkins Brown's *Homespun Heroines*, indicating that she was familiar with some of the women actively writing during the Harlem Renaissance. She cites these sources even though black scholarship enjoyed little recognition by the white academy.

The thesis is divided into five chapters on the legal, social, religious, economic, and educational status of the African-American female. The first chapter analyzes English and American legal documents (colonial charters, early state constitutions, and legislation) governing the slave trade and enslaved people. Later chapters focus on testimonies (oral histories) of female survivors of slavery and Reconstruction. "I feel," writes Gordon, "that citing some of the stories told by slave women themselves will do much to establish a fair idea of [their] social position during that period" (46). A quotation from the work of white abolitionist and feminist Angelina Grimké Weld (Harlem Renaissance writer and great-aunt of Angelina Weld Grimké) and *The Anti-Slavery Examiner* describes an enslaved girl "who was sent to the workhouse to be flogged, and who was accordingly stripped naked and whipped, leaving deep gashes on her back large enough to insert one's finger where the flesh had been cut out by the torturing lashes" (38). One is left to imagine the reaction of Gordon's white male thesis committee when such vivid testimony of cruelties was placed before them.

With clarity and dispassion, Gordon explains that at the outset slavery was not allowed by charters of the English colonies, but was legalized by state constitutions. In this way Gordon exposes slavery and its sequel, institutionalized racism, as peculiar social constructs: "After 1678, slavery was recognized in the colonies [Northern and Southern] both by statute and by common law decisions" (8). She cites a 1619 legal case as the beginning of the Negro woman being classified in the same category as property, livestock, or runaway dogs (10). The sheer weight of the evidence that Gordon presents cannot have failed to impress her readers with the enormity of the suffering endured by black women and the heroic resistance they exhibited at every turn.

That Gordon's analysis is also feminist should be obvious. In the sense that she differentiates between two kinds of oppression—one that is racist and another that is at once racist and sexist—she anticipates more recent black feminist writing that builds on such insight. Yet she does not emphasize gender-based oppression to the exclusion of the male experience. Writes Gordon, "Much of the material in this thesis is applicable to Negro men as well as to Negro women as it must be remembered that for three hundred years, under both chattel slavery and wage slavery, Negro women worked under the same conditions as the men. [However, i]n addition to being a slave, the Negro woman was subjected to the double handicap of being a Negro and at the same time being a woman and was prostituted to the lust of the slave-holders" (1).

Gordon shows her awareness of the complexity of such matters, admitting that white women also suffered poverty and discrimination, that not all white behavior was evil ("many masters maintained schools for their mulatto children"), and that black complicity in slavery existed in some cases as well ("a Charlestown Negro who purchased his wife for seven hundred dollars sold her at a profit of fifty dollars because she misbehaved" (32).

In the summary of her thesis (pp. 83–87) Gordon moves away from its predominant technical emphasis and reveals her own attitudes about her theme. She has this to say about the sexual harassment and exploitation from which black women, as opposed in white women in the South, had no recourse:

> The Negro woman's position was one of peril; she was subjected to
> a double moral standard, one for her and one for her white sister.

The Negro woman was not protected by law, nor by public opinion, against the sexual passion and pursuit of the southern white "gentlemen." (87)

In showing that the black female lacked the protection granted to white women, Gordon was addressing "the cult of true womanhood," defined and analyzed by Hazel Carby five decades later (1987).[21] She also anticipates the analyses offered by Gloria Wade-Gayles, bell hooks, and many other black feminists who address issues of double oppression.

A great deal more research is required to assess or fully comprehend the import of Edythe Mae Gordon's life and writing. A narrative of her life must be crafted with close attention to gaps; her work must be analyzed in the fuller context of black writing by both men and women during the period. Each detail is part of a larger puzzle that needs to be thoroughly reconstructed before a picture can emerge of one black woman's life and work. The arduous task of documenting the life and career of invisible writers like Edythe Mae Gordon should be carried out by researchers sensitive to issues of race, gender, and political ideology. Only then can this chapter of the American experience be delivered from obscurity. The writings of black women must be sought out in all possible locations, to be identified, documented, classified, and commented upon without prior assumptions or preconceived agendas, with the realization that it is the black writer who should have spoken and written her life, told her own tale. If she did not, we must ask "How might she have told her tale?" and "What terrible secrets was she guarding by ending her life in silence?"[22]

NOTES

[1]"Buried Deep," in Beatrice M. Murphy, ed., *Negro Voices: An Anthology of Contemporary Verse* (New York: Henry Harrison Poetry Publisher, 1938), 66.

[2]*The Living Is Easy* (Boston: Houghton Mifflin, 1948). West, who authored numerous short stories in the 1920s, published *The Living Is Easy* only after the Harlem Renaissance waned. She has recently surprised the reading public with a second novel, *The Wedding* (New York: Doubleday, 1995).

[3]The *Cumulative Index* for *Opportunity: Journal of Negro Life, Volumes 1–27 (1923–1949)* lists no poems by Gordon. I have not located any by leafing through the pages of the journal either.

[4]National Archives, Waltham, Massachusetts.

[5]Other black women writers of the Harlem Renaissance who subtracted from their ages were Zora Neale Hurston, Dorothy West, and Nella Larsen.

[6]Given a birth date of 1896, Edythe Mae Gordon may have graduated from the M Street (High) School with the class of 1913 or 1914. In 1916 the school moved around the corner and was renamed Dunbar High School.

[7]Sandra Fitzpatrick and Maria R. Goodwin, *The Guide to Black Washington: Places and Events of Historical and Cultural Significance in the Nation's Capital* (New York: Hippocrene Books, 1990).

[8]A photograph of Professor Morris with his Model T Ford appears in "The Hub" calendar for 1925, with the caption "Professor Morris feeding oatmeal to his flivver." See Kathleen Kilgore, *Transformations: A History of Boston University* (Boston: Boston University Press, 1991), 156, n. 20.

[9]In 1940 the School of Religious Education became the School of Social Work. The new school was established "to increase contributions to community welfare in Massachusetts and New England." Kilgore, op. cit.

[10]Election Commission, City of Cambridge, Massachusetts.

[11]Boston city directories, Boston Public Library, Boston, Massachusetts.

[12]See note 1.

[13]This information proved useful for locating her in the Census records, where her birth date appears as June 6, 1896. Her name is spelled "Edith" Chapman (with no middle name).

[14]Some of Eugene Gordon's papers are held in the manuscript division of the Schomburg Center for Research in Black Culture in New York City.

[15]Workers Library Publishers, P.O.B. 148, Station D, New York, NY, February 1935.

[16]*The Crusader: Official Organ of the African Blood Brotherhood and the Hamitic League of the World, 1918–1922*, ed. Cyril V. Briggs. A Facsimile of the Periodical, edited and with a new introduction and index by Robert A. Hill (New York: Garland, 1987).

[17]Obituary of Eugene Gordon, *Daily World*, Friday, March 22, 1974.

[18]June Gordon, born Sonia Crowll in Odessa (1901), who like her husband was a member of the Communist party, fought a deportation order entered against her on August 6, 1960, by the Immigration and Naturalization Service of the United States. *New York Times*, August 6, 1960.

[19]Arthur M. Schlesinger, Jr., *The Crisis of the Old Order*, 1937, quoted in Harvey Swados, ed., *The American Writer and the Great Depression* (Indianapolis: Bobbs Merrill, 1966).

[20]Census records for Washington, DC, in 1900 list Edythe Mae Chapman's grandmother Matilda Bicks, a laundress, as head of household. She could neither read nor write. The other members of the household were Matilda Bicks's daughters, Mary S. Bicks, born in 1879 (Edythe's mother), and Elizabeth Bicks, born in 1884. Both Mary and Elizabeth list their occupation as "servant."

[21]Hazel Carby, *Reconstructing Womanhood*, chapter "Slave and Mistress."

[22]I acknowledge with gratitude the valuable assistance of Charlie Niles, Special Collections librarian, Mugar Memorial Library, Boston University; the Office of the Registrar at Boston University; Betty Gubert, Research Librarian, Schomburg Center for Research in Black Culture, New York; Joan Stockard, Research Librarian at Wellesley College; Professor Maryemma Graham and her students Sharon Pineault Burke and Eileen Kennedy at Northeastern University; Edward Wotis; McConarty; Ruth E. Randolph; and Jonathan Leigh Roses.

FICTION

Edythe Mae Gordon. Courtesy of Boston University Archives

[2]

HOSTESS

By EDYTHE MAE GORDON

H ELLO, ANGEL FACE." Tom, heavy, brown-skinned, and
wearing a gray-checked suit, strolled toward a girl seated alone at
one of the tables. "Hello yourself, big boy." Mazie scrutinized him
for a moment above the rim of her hand mirror, then continued to
dab suntan powder on her thin, pert, yellow face.

"What say, kid, we get married? How 'bout it, girlie?" Tom
grinned engagingly.

Mazie gave her features a final inspection and replaced the mirror in her beaded bag. She brushed his suggestion aside with a
wave of her small hand.

"Ah, can that stuff. You know you ain't the marrying kind. What
you trying to do, kid me or something?" She laughed shortly.

The orchestra began wailing and Mazie and Tom melted into
the swaying mass on the dance floor. Once she put her hand to
her bag to feel whether she had the small bottle of sleeping potion.
The doctor who prescribed it had warned her to be careful; an
overdose would be fatal.

In the early morning, after long hours of boosting Eddie
Mason's trade by drinking and dancing with those men who had
no partners, she was too tired and too nervous to sleep. . . .

Mazie lay abed staring into space. The clock on the church
nearby struck ten. The warm sun bathed her tired face. There were
deep circles beneath her large, drooping eyes; tiny lines about her
mouth that were discernible only on close inspection. She shivered and pulled the silk, wool-filled puff about her slim shoulders.

Her black hair lay in ringlets about her face and her full breasts
rose and fell with growing excitement. For a long time she had
been thinking critically of herself. What a little fool she had been

to leave Jack, her husband. What a fool to run away with "Saxophone" Bill. He had fascinated her; she had lost her head and left Jack to follow him. Jack had given her everything—a house, expensively furnished, luxurious clothes, jewels. . . .

He had not, however, given her the companionship and attention that she craved. She had desired someone like a red-hot sheik from Harlem. She had not appreciated Jack's sincerity and devotion. She had wanted a man with a line.

Lettie, her best girl friend, had told her to be more discreet; not to carry the affair with Bill too far. Lettie was not much for looks, but she had lots of sex appeal and she knew how to get what she wanted. She advised Mazie not to try the patience of her husband too much, or some day she would regret her little gaiety. Lettie's admonition had made no impression, of course. If anything, it had made Mazie more determined to do as she pleased. She had felt that she had a right to live. She was going to enjoy life. She was going to live. She was going to drink it all in.

She marveled at Bill's curly hair, his soft, tapering fingers, his pensive eyes. Bill had pulled her close to him. He had put his arms around her and she had been thrilled. He would play some sentimental thing and her heart would behave shamefully. The tones of his saxophone mingled with her pent-up feelings. Time after time he told her that he could no longer live without her, and begged her to go away with him.

Mazie packed her clothes one day and left. She wrote a short note to Jack and pinned it to the dresser cover. She had no qualms of conscience. True, she had taken all the jewels Jack had given her and all her clothes, but she had not taken one cent of his money. She took her own, and felt independent, free to indulge her whims and desires.

Mazie and Bill traveled. They went everywhere, finally ending back in Harlem. Bill's sensitive, artistic nature unfitted him for work. They played around cabarets and night clubs until Mazie's money had vanished. One morning she awoke to find Bill gone. It was soon afterwards that she took the job as hostess at Eddie Mason's night club. . . .

Mazie lay abed staring into space. Her excitement had not abated, but she had definitely made up her mind. She'd go back to

Jack. She'd ask his forgiveness. She'd go and tell him what a fool she had been. One thing about him, he had always been broad-minded. He was one person in the world who'd understand. She'd tell him of how Bill had deserted her when her money was gone. The yellow dog.

She was out of the bed now. She gathered her underclothes from the dresser drawers and dress from hangers in the closet, stuffing them all recklessly into her bags. She then combed her hair, meanwhile scrutinizing herself in the mirror. She knew she looked tired and older, so she plastered red on her cheeks and rouged her lips. She pulled a small red felt hat on her well-shaped head and drew a fur scarf around her neck. She didn't look half bad, and knew it.

Hastening into the street she hailed a taxi-cab, giving an address in the Bronx. She leaned back on the soiled upholstery and tried to imagine what Jack would say. He'd, of course, show surprise. He'd be angry at first, but she'd tell him how sorry she was for leaving him. He loved her. He'd forgive her. He was very understanding. She was cured. She knew the value of things now. She had learned her lesson, all right. She'd not been fair to Jack. She remembered how she had met him while she was working as a salesgirl in Beck's bargain basement store. She recalled how he had fallen in love with her. He had been so different from the other men she had known. He had told her that he loved her. He wanted to marry her. He wanted to take her out of the bargain basement and give her a chance to enjoy life. He wanted to protect her.

She gazed out the window. Raindrops whirled themselves softly against the glass. Hot tears came to her eyes. She thought what a cheat she had been. . . . And a failure. . . . And what a mess she had made of everything. If Jack would take her back she'd never, never, never. . . . After he had forgiven her she would tell about the child she expected in a few months. . . . She *knew* Jack would understand. All this. . . . in less than eleven months.

The taxi stopped at the door of a red-brick house that loomed three stories close to the sidewalk. She got out, paid the driver, and mounted the gray stone steps hesitantly. She opened the door and walked into the hall which led into the large parlor and into the library. She saw Jack immediately, where he was seated in a big leather chair in the library, facing her. She set her bags down and stood just within the door, observing him. He looked at her, his hands clinching the arms of the chair, but his face showing neither surprise nor anger.

He said simply: "Oh, you're back?" There was a cutting edge to his voice.

She saw the dining-room table beyond the door of the library and caught her breath as odors of food reached her from the kitchen.

"Yes. He left me, Jack, and I've come back to beg you to forgive me . . . to take me back. Oh, Jack, I love you! You know . . ." Emotion choked her and her voice was broken by sobs.

She stood watching for a sign from him. But he had not moved. So she approached and laid her hand on his shoulder. . . . The table was laid for two.

"Why, you going to have company to lunch, Jack?" She looked at him reproachfully and turned back toward her bags.

"I'll go up and dress, Jack. Have the cook set another place."

Still gazing at her, fascinated, he shook his head slowly.

"I'm afraid you wouldn't care to stay, Mazie. You see, it's my wife who is my guest. She's upstairs dressing now. You remember Lettie, your old friend? Well, we were married yesterday." There was no regret in his voice, no emotion of any kind: it was calm, commonplace, matter of fact.

Mazie's face burned and a flood of rebellious words died on her lips, unspoken. She stood with her mouth open. Then she backed out the room to the door. With a bag dangling in each hand she went wearily into the street.

That night at Eddie Mason's she told Tom she'd go with him. This was her last fight against herself. The music blared. As she danced her red georgette evening dress flowed gracefully about her. A flood of recollections poured into her mind, the force of them making her sway, and the memory of everything she once loved entered into a merciless conspiracy to punish her.

She and Tom sat down at a table and he ordered drinks.

"Here's to a love that'll never end." He saluted her with his glass, then turned it up to his lips. It was then that she slipped some of the sleeping potion into her glass. She drank . . .

A strange quietness fell upon Mazie and the red lights cast shadows over her worn face. She slumped in her chair.

Tom stared. He called:

"Oh, my God, Mazie's dying!"

They carried her limp body out and laid it on a couch in the back room.

IF WISHES
WERE HORSES

BY EDYTHE MAE GORDON

THE BOAT CHURNED its way up the harbor. Men, women and children filled the decks. Numbers of people sat on folding chairs. The wind blew fiercely. Women held down their skirts to keep their knees from showing.

In the shadows, near a corner, there sat a man holding the hand of a little girl. His brown felt hat flopped weakly over a sallow, hollow-cheeked face. He stroked his greying black hair with an impatient gesture. His harassed mind had been further disturbed. What had that gypsy fortune-teller meant, anyway? For the fun of it, he had gone into her tent on the beach. Now he could not dismiss from his mind this swarthy, dirty-looking woman in her outlandish costume of red, orange, and purple.

He got up and went below. He bought himself a magazine, and a bar of candy for the little girl. On their way up, they stopped to watch the greenish-white water dash angrily against the huge wheels.

The boat passed an island, and most of the passengers rose, went to the railing, and stretched their necks in an effort to see the prisoners the city kept there. Fred Pomeroy sat down. He was wretched in his dejection. His only interest lay in trying to fathom the meaning of the fortune-teller's prognostication. She had taken his hand and examined the lines of its palm. After several minutes, she had said:

"Things will be different. Your wife will be able to realize her desires. She'll do some of the things that she has long wished to do. You'll be the maker of her dreams."

Frowning, he glanced down at his trousers. Though neatly pressed, they were noticeably threadbare. They had been in service for three years. He had worked for five years in Shannon-Jones' Department Store, selling yards and yards of muslin to tired and irritable women. At night he wrote stories. He did not make much advancement at the department store. As to the stories, all he had been able to realize from them were pink, blue, and white rejection slips. Perhaps there was a check at home for the story "Love Will Find a Way," sent to "Love Art" magazine. Or perhaps, tomorrow morning, he'd get a promotion, with a ten-dollar raise, at Shannon-Jones'.

He gazed absently at Dorothea, who had slipped from his embrace. She was playing with a little boy on the deck. Pomeroy looked at her, but he was thinking, "What does it all mean?" He wondered why he had gone into the gypsy's tent at all. Why had he been attracted to "Madam Lenora," this woman who guaranteed to read one's entire life—the past, the present and the future—declaring that one would be wiser and happier after a visit to her?

"True," he reflected, "in a way. She did tell me something, but she read neither my past nor my present. She only told me of my future. I am not happier; certainly I am not wiser. I can't see how *I* can make Rachel's dreams come true, when I don't know what they are, even."

Pomeroy's mazagine dangled between his slim, brittle fingers. He pondered, and his mood created these lines:

> Why are we always groping,—
> Why are we always hoping
> To obliterate the pain
> And happiness to attain?

When he walked from the boat down the gang-plank to the wharf, leading Dorothea by the hand, his eyes strayed to a poster:

EXCURSION DATES

If Wishes Were Horses

CONSULT C. J. MANIX
Proprietor of the Beautiful Steamer
QUEEN MARY
SUNDAY EXCURSIONS
2:30 and 6:30 p. m.
Come early and make your reservations

Pomeroy made a grimace, grasped Dorothea's hand, and hurried away. He was tired of excursions. He never wanted to see a beach again.

Rachel's critical eyes noticed how listless her husband was at dinner. He ate but little, and complained as usual of feeling ill. She attributed his lackadaisical manner to fatigue. He seemed to be tired, exhausted, all the time.

They had been in bed for hours when Rachel awoke. She felt cold air blowing upon her, and she pulled the covers closer. Yet she shivered. She had dreamed that she was flying alone in an airplane. She had been sitting in the cockpit with perfect control, when, suddenly, something had gone wrong and the engine had died. The plane had plunged down into emptiness. It had struck an ice peak and had landed on a glaciated mountain. She had heard a roaring noise and had seen a huge block of ice split itself from the glacier. She had been unable to reach the wrecked plane because of the faceted spurs. No human being had been in sight . . . Her feet were freezing. She lay shivering.

She lay thus for several seconds. She felt colder all the time. It occurred to her that the room was as void of sound as the arctic wastes had been. She listened to hear her husband's breathing. There was no sound. Suddenly afraid, she reached out her hand and laid it on his face. He was icy cold . . .

Some weeks later Rachel received a long blue envelope in the mail. When she opened it a check for $50,000 fell on her lap.

It was Pomeroy's insurance . . .

Nellie Niles, who had once lived across the street from the Pomeroys, sat reading the Sunday newspapers.

She idly turned to the society section. For the amusement it afforded her, she read column after column concerning marriages, bridge parties, weddings, club activities, church affairs, and the doings of the younger set. Her eyes came to rest on the headline:

SAILS FOR EUROPE

She read the accompanying story:

Mrs. Alfred Pomeroy, of 69 Academy road, Boston, accompanied by her daughter, Dorothea, sailed Friday afternoon for Europe. After touring Italy, France, and Spain, Mrs. Pomeroy will be the guest of Mrs. Conklin Van Bruce, at her villa at Cap D'all, France.

Nellie Niles stared from protruding eyes, then she read the item over again, slowly. She laid the sheet on her knees, her heart beating painfully and her gaze straying off into space.

She sighed. In an acrimonious tone, she exclaimed aloud: "Gee, gosh!" Then she added mournfully: "Some people have all the luck!"

SUBVERSION

By EDYTHE MAE GORDON

THE DEEPENING TWILIGHT wrapped the world in a dusky veil of mystery. Like a tired runner, the wind sighed among the bare branches overhead. Houses and stores, people and automobiles, streets and sidewalks, all sank into indistinguishable shadow.

John Marley was a music teacher—a teacher of piano, and an unsuccessful one. His face was deeply furrowed, and the coat which he pulled protectingly about him was threadbare. In his tired, muddy eyes there lay a puzzled expression. Where was he to get the money to pay the note that was due? An immense self-pity gripped his throat.

He again ran over in his mind his most likely friends. . . . Suddenly his muddy eyes grew clearer. How had he forgotten Charlie Delany?

Delany was a bachelor, and, incidentally, a prosperous realtor.

"No luck this year," muttered John Marley.

He stumbled with an uncertain gait up Broad street on his way to Delany's house.

"I've never asked him for anything," the music teacher thought. "And we've been good to him. . . . No luck this year. No luck any year. The doctor said one lung's gone. Maybe I won't live long, anyway. I bet my wife will be glad. I'm a miserable failure. . . . Then she'll have some money . . . my insurance."

When he reached the intersection of Broad and Waverly streets he slipped and fell on the sidewalk. Automobiles whizzed by. A crowd gathered. John Marley looked foolish. He turned his head round to see who had noticed him fall. He shuffled to his feet. A few yards away in the street lay his hat. He picked it up and smoothed out the folds made by the automobile. As he buttoned up his coat, he shivered and continued on his way.

"What's happened to you, Marley?" Charlie Delany asked, opening the door wide. He slapped Marley gently on the shoulder as he propelled his friend into the warm living room.

"Slipped on the icy sidewalk. Got all wet." John Marley looked ruefully at himself, then went over and stood in front of the sizzling radiator.

"Too bad! You can't go out in this condition . . . a wet coat. Take mine. I'll get it later." Charlie Delany's coat was of black broadcloth with collar, cuffs, and lining of soft beaver.

Finally, several bills of large denomination having been pressed into Marley's hand, he prepared to go. He said:

"Don't forget Lena and I expect you to dinner tomorrow, as usual." Being assured that Charlie would be present, he shut the door with vigor and departed.

Charlie Delany was an old friend. Since he was not married he always ate Thanksgiving dinner with the Marleys. They would not think of having him eat dinner in a restaurant on Thanksgiving Day.

On his way home Marley gradually began to see things in a different light. Life seemed a bit more cheerful. His cough seemed less painful. Perhaps it was Charlie Delany's beaverlined coat, with the beaver collar and cuffs, that made him feel different. One would feel different in a warm coat. Charlie Delany had given him a glass of gin—"to heat you up and keep you from catching more cold." It did more, for it enkindled in him the fire of renewed manhood.

Why didn't he get a good warm coat? Didn't clothes help determine what people thought of you? Didn't you have to be the master of your own fate? If he had had a warm coat three years ago perhaps he'd have two strong lungs today. People didn't want him teaching their children when he was continually coughing. And he could not blame them. From one of the easy-payment stores he could get a fairly good coat. Ten dollars down and a dollar a week. . . .

He straightened his shoulders and almost strutted up Broad street. When he reached a brilliantly-lighted store, whose window displayed a variety of merchandise, he turned the knob smartly and sauntered importantly through the door. He felt happy, and he must buy something for Lena. He wanted to make her happy, too. From the variety of things in the store he finally decided upon a pretty but inexpensive scarf for Lena and a toy airplane for the boy.

He hoped the scarf would please his wife. Perhaps she would show him more affection. Perhaps she would not be quite so cold. He remembered how Lena had loved him before worries came, before the cough came, before slender times came. After all, who knew but that the doctor might be mistaken? He might live a long time. One could live quite a long while with one lung. He might even increase the number of his pupils, if he tried hard enough. He would then have more money . . . Lena would then love him as she had long ago.

He thought: "Lena used to quarrel every time I invited Charlie Delany to dinner. She'd make mean remarks. Gradually she changed her attitude toward him. Why shouldn't she change her attitude toward me, and love me again if I am more prosperous?"

John Marley went to one or two other places, among them the barber shop. He got a haircut and had his face massaged. It was eight o'clock when at last he reached home.

He was thinking, as he mounted the steps:

"What will Lena say when she sees me wearing this beautiful coat? She'll brighten up and run up to me and kiss me, I'll bet." He paused in the dark hall. He put his hand into the coat pocket for the key but it was in his own old coat, and that was at Charlie Delany's. He rang the bell. In the dark hall Lena gave him a kiss and put her arms about his neck. She stood very close to him and stroked the beaver collar. She kissed him again and again and buried her head against the coat, now cooing softly:

"Marley isn't home, yet. The boy cried and called for you today."

Keen knife-thrust was Lena's voice. How weary he felt! How useless was life! How futile everything!

"Yes," answered John Marley, his voice striving treacherously to betray him. He kissed her tenderly. "Yes, he's home."

At dinner next day John Marley sat very quiet. At the table Lena tried hard to act as if everything was all right. One who noticed would have plainly seen that she was ill with fear. She wondered what her husband was thinking. She wished she had a chance to tell Charlie of last night.

While Charlie talked and laughed over his own stories, John sat staring at his son. He thought he saw Charlie's eyes and chin. Lena, Charlie, and the child ate. The husband hoped they did not notice him. He wondered what Lena thought, but could not look at her.

"You seem very quiet today, John." Charlie reached for the after-dinner mints. "Thinking about the accident of last night, I guess," he hazarded, sympathetically.

"Yes." John pushed back his chair, putting his hand to his mouth as if to hide the convulsive tremor of his lips.

"I'm thinking about my boy!" There was a pause, then he continued:

"I'm thinking of something else, too. I don't believe I'm going to live much longer. Life has given me all the joy it ever will."

As he spoke a vague incomprehensible solitude encompassed him.

"I want to thank you for your friendship, Charlie. When I'm gone be kind to Lena and the boy. I can think of no more appropriate person to ask such a favor of."

Charlie Delany mumbled incoherently and was vividly red in the face. He looked away. Lena's eyes were twice their usual size. She acted as if she was going to cry.

NONFICTION

BOSTON UNIVERSITY

GRADUATE SCHOOL

THESIS

THE STATUS OF THE NEGRO WOMAN IN THE UNITED STATES

FROM 1619–1865

BY

EDYTHE MAE GORDON

(B. S. IN S. S., BOSTON UNIVERSITY, 1934.)

SUBMITTED IN PARTIAL FULFILLMENT OF THE REQUIREMENTS FOR THE
DEGREE OF MASTER OF ARTS

1935

[19]

TABLE OF CONTENTS

PREFACE

The aims of this thesis are to indicate some of the important facts concerning the Negro woman in the United States between the years of 1619 and 1865, which will help to determine her status during that period, to supply the necessary historical background needed for the study of this nature, and to stimulate further study in this neglected field of Negro history.

It is my intention to set forth the legalistic viewpoint, which gives the theoretical treatment of the Negro woman, and to follow this with material which will show the actual treatment and her status in my analyses.

The material presented here has not been treated before in this form with the view of establishing the status of the Negro woman in one volume from the five points of view given: the legal, the social, the religious, the economic, and the educational.

Much of the material in this thesis is applicable to Negro men as well as to Negro women as it must be remembered that for three hundred years, under both chattel slavery and wage slavery, Negro women worked under the same conditions as the men. In addition to being a slave, the Negro woman was subjected to the double handicap of being a Negro and at the same time being a woman and was prostituted to the lust of the slave-holders.

I try to point out that in spite of all the obstacles, some progress was made during that period, and that the Negro woman has played a heroic role which has been measured by patience, endurance, self-sacrifice and love. Even in those dark days prior to emancipation, she made her contribution to American civilization.

In the summary, I try, in as concise a manner as possible, to epitomize the material given in the body of the thesis. This is done with the hope of leaving a vivid picture of the struggles, cruelties, inhumanities and injustices to which the Negro woman was a victim under the system of chattel slavery which lasted for nearly three hundred years. Also, I suggest the present day situation of the Negro woman, and intimate a remedy.

I. THE LEGAL STATUS OF THE NEGRO WOMAN

1. COLONIAL CHARTERS.

In order to determine the legal status of the Negro woman in the United States from 1619–1865, it is first necessary to review the different charters of the colonies.

Most of the English colonies were under charters granted by the crown of England. They destinated the limits of the colonies' territory and the extent of their powers of self-government. These charters changed and amended from time to time.

Sir Walter Raleigh in 1584 was granted the first charter,[1] It gave him the authority to make settlements within certain limits, and granted to him and to his heirs and assigns the privilege of making all statutes, laws, and ordinances for the government of any colony. The statutes, laws, and ordinances must be agreeable to the form of the laws, statutes, government or to the policy of England.

The first charter of Virginia[2] was issued in 1606. This charter granted to the colonies the right to be governed according to such laws, as shall be in that behalf, given and signed with the King's hand, and passed under the Privy Seal of the King of England. Later in 1609, the second charter of Virginia[3] granted the colonists the right to punish, pardon, and rule according to such orders, ordinances, constitutions, directions and instructions as by our said council, as shall be established, and in cases of capital and criminal law, it shall be agreeable to the laws, statutes, government and policy of the Realm of England.

---

1. Poore's *Constitutions,* p. 1381.
2. Ibid., p. 1890.
3. Ibid., p. 1901.

In 1611–1612, the third and last charter of Virginia[1] granted the full power and authority to ordain and make such laws and ordinances for the good and welfare of the said plantation, and such laws and statutes shall not be contrary to the Realm of England.

The same provisions were in all of the other charters, with slight variations that no laws, statutes, government shall be established which are contrary to the policy of England. The charter issued in 1620 to the New England Company[2] granted to the council of the company full power and authority to make, ordain and establish all manner of orders, laws, directions, constitutions, forms and ceremonies of government and magistracy, fit and necessary for and concerning the government of the said colony and plantation, which should not be contrary to the Realm of England.

In 1629, the first charter of the Massachusetts Bay Colony[3] gave to the colony assembled with the Governor or Lieutenant Governor the same powers; that is, such laws and statutes not contrary to the laws of the Realm of England. The second charter of Massachusetts Bay[4] grants similar privileges and powers. No alteration in this clause was made in the Explanatory Charter of Massachusetts Bay in 1726.[5]

Captain John Mason, his heirs and assigns by the grant of New Hampshire in 1629,[1] were empowered to establish a government which shall have power to govern agreeably, as near as may be, to the laws of the Realm of England. Full judicial and administrative authority was given to New Hampshire by the grant of 1635.[2] By the royal commission appointed in 1680,[3] the New Hampshire colony was to be governed by the judgment of the council sitting

---

1. Poore's *Constitutions*, p. 1905.
2. Ibid., p. 925.
3. Ibid., p. 937.
4. Ibid., p. 951.
5. Ibid., p. 954.
1. Poore's *Constitutions*, p. 127.
2. Ibid., p. 1274.
3. Ibid., p. 1276.

as a Court of Record, and to be as nearly as possible in accordance with the laws and statutes of the Realm of England.

The Charter of Maryland[4] granted similar powers. In 1662, the Charter of Connecticut[5] empowered the governor and six assistants to make, ordain, and establish laws, statutes, ordinances not contrary to the law of England.

All law making was placed in the hands of Sir Ferdinando Gorges, his heirs and assigns by the grant of the Province of Maine in 1639,[6] in order that the same ordinances be not contrary to the laws and statutes of the Kingdom of England. The same restrictions were included in the grants of Maine in 1664 and 1674 to the Duke of York.[7] The Providence Plantation received full power to make all laws and ordinances by the patent of 1643.[8]

The charter of Rhode Island and Providence Plantation in 1663 gave the governor and assistants the same power.[9] Similar power was granted by the charter of Pennsylvania by Charles II to William Penn and subject to the same limitations. The charters of Pennsylvania in 1701[10] and Georgia's in 1632[11] gave to the corporation power to form and to prepare laws, statutes, and ordinances fit and necessary for the government of said colonies, not repugnant to the laws of England.

In 1663 and 1665, Carolina charters[1] vested in the proprietors of the province with the consent of the freemen the right to make all ordinances which were agreeable to the laws and customs of the Realm of England. John Locke drew up the Fundamental Constitution of Carolina in 1669; this was repealed in 1693; the first and only allusion to slaves or to slavery was made in this constitution. Section 107 states: "Since charity obliges us to wish well to the souls of all men and religion ought to alter nothing in

---

4. Ibid., p. 813.
5. Ibid., p. 255.
6. Ibid., p. 777.
7. Ibid., p. 784.
8. Ibid., p. 1595.
9. Poore's *Constitutions*, p. 1598.
10. Ibid., pp. 1540; 273.
11. Ibid., p. 374.
1. Poore's *Constitutions*, pp. 1382; 1384

any man's civil estate or rights, it shall be lawful for slaves, as well as others, to enter themselves, and be of what church or profession any of them shall think best, and, therefore be as fully members as any freeman. But yet no slave shall hereby be exempted from the civil dominion that his master hath over him, but in all things in the same state and condition he was in before."[2] Section 110 states: "Every freeman of Carolina shall have absolute power and authority over his Negro slaves of what opinion or religion soever."[3]

2. ENGLISH LAW.

We find conflicting opinions, upon examining the English cases, as to the rights of masters over the persons of their slaves while in England. In the earlier cases, the contention was that such rights were continued. The cases were usually based upon Negroes who had run away or who had been taken away from their masters. In the twenty-ninth year of Charles II, the first of these cases appeared. Action was sustained on the ground of the custom of merchants in the colonies. The next case for trover[1] was the fourth year of William and Mary; at this time the court was of the opinion that trover would not lie, while in the fifth year of William and Mary it was held that the Negro might be a slave as he was considered to be a heathen and trover would therefore lie.

In the seventh year of William and Mary, it was declared that while slavery was not legal in England, the colonies could make laws establishing slavery as a local custom as this prevailed in some parts of England.

In the term of the twelfth year of George III, occurred the case of James Somersett. Somersett who had been made a slave in Africa was sold there, and brought to Virginia where he was again sold. His new master later took him to England, where he escaped. Recaptured, he was confined upon a ship of a Captain Knowles. Lord Mansfield issued a writ of Habeas Corpus, and since the

---

2. Ibid., p. 1407.
3. Ibid., p. 1408.
1. Trover was an action to recover the value of personal property of the plaintiff wrongfully withheld or converted by another to his own use.

court was not of the opinion that the return was sufficient for enslavement, the Negro was released. Lord Mansfield said: "The state of slavery is of such a nature that it is incapable of being introduced on any reasons, moral or political, but only positive law, which preserves its force long after reasons, occasions, and time itself, from which it was created, is erased from memory. It is so odious, that nothing can be suffered to support it, but positive law. Whatever inconveniences, therefore, may follow from a decision, I cannot say this case is allowed or approved by the laws of England, and therefore the blacks must be discharged."[1]

After 1678, slavery was recognized in the colonies both by statute and by common law decisions.[2] Until then, it would seem that slavery was illegal, unless it could be held to have arisen by prescription, and such an idea would apparently be controverted by the decision of Lord Mansfield. Hence the conclusion that slavery though practiced was illegal.

3. IMPORTATION OF NEGROES IN THE COLONIES.

A cargo of twenty Africans were landed from a Dutch man-of-war at Jamestown, Virginia, in August 1619.[3] With this introduction of Negroes in Virginia, slavery gradually made its way into all the thirteen colonies, and was sanctioned by their several legislatures. Although slavery was not originally established by law, nor did it legally exist, slavery actually existed, resting wholly upon the sanction of custom, and then laws were required to control it. The acts first passed in Virginia were merely regulations for servants.[4] On December 14, 1662, the Civil law rule as to descent was adopted. Eight years later, October 3, 1670, servants who were not Christians imported by shipping were declared slaves for life. Slavery in Virginia was thus legalized.

It is important to note that until 1664 Negroes in Virginia and other colonies were not slaves but indentured servants. The twenty

---

1. See West, G. M., *Status of the Negro in Virginia.*
2. Ibid.
3. Cromwell, *The Negro in American History*, p. 3.
4. The legal distinction between servants and slaves was that servants were immigrants serving a term of years under indenture and immigrant servants serving for life were slaves.

Africans brought over on a Dutch man-of-war at Jamestown, were not slaves; they were put to work for the government as indentured servants.

Incidentally, slaves were first mentioned by a proposed law of 1638, four years after its settlement. The Dutch gave it first legal recognition in Delaware in 1721, although it had really existed in the colony since 1666.

At the time of the establishment of the colony in Georgia, slavery was prohibited by Oglethrope in 1733, but the prohibition was repealed in 1749 and the first legislation recognizing slavery as an institution was in 1755.[1]

The Dutch brought slavery into New Jersey, and received legal recognition in 1664. While New York was a Dutch colony of New Netherlands in 1626, slavery was introduced and received legal recognition in 1665.[2] Importation was never directly established in Connecticut by statute, and the time of the introduction of slavery is unknown.[3] Slavery in Massachusetts was recognized in 1633. A Salem ship began the importation of slaves from the West Indies in 1836, and was forbidden in the fundamental law in 1641. By acts of 1714 and 1718, the statutes of New Hampshire show two legal recognitions of slavery. These acts were to regulate the conduct of servants and slaves and masters.

Although there were some differences between slavery in the North and in the South, attributable to economic rather than moral causes, the legal status was the same.[1]

The General Assembly of Virginia in 1778 enacted that "no slaves shall hereafter be imported into this commonwealth, by sea or land, nor shall any slave or slaves so imported be sold or brought by any person whatsoever," under penalty of one thousand pounds for every slave imported and fined a hundred pounds for every one either sold or bought, and the slave himself to be free. It was also provided that persons removing to the state from

---

1. Cromwell, op. cit., p. 3.
2. Ibid., p. 4.
3. Ibid., p. 4.
1. Collins, H. W., *The Domestic Trade of the Southern States*, p. 110.

other states with the intention of becoming citizens of Virginia might bring their slaves with them.

This act did not apply to persons claiming slaves by descent, marriage, or divorce, or to any citizen of Virginia who was then the actual owner of slaves within the United States, nor to transients with slave attendants.[2]

A law was enacted in 1785 declaring to free the slaves who would afterwards be imported and kept in the State a year, whether at one time or at several times. The same exceptions were made to this law as in the law of 1778.

In 1796, these acts were amended; thus it was made lawful for any citizen of the United States residing in Virginia or owning lands there, to carry out any slaves born in the state and bring them back. If they were entitled to freedom in the state to which they moved, they could not be held as slaves in Virginia again.[3]

A law was passed in 1806 which prohibited the introduction of slaves into Virginia.[1] In 1811 the law was amended to restore to residents of the state the privilege concerning the importation of slaves which they had under the law in 1778. The act was further amended to extend the right to immigrants to bring in slaves. Those importing slaves were required to exhibit before a justice of the peace a written statement with the name, age, sex and description of each slave. The law of 1819 permitted the importation of slaves not convicted of crime from any section of the United States.

South Carolina, in 1792, passed a law to prohibit for two years the importation of slaves from Africa or from "other places beyond the seas." It also prohibited slaves in the United States who were bound by a term of years. As the act was revised in 1794 and 1797, it prohibited the introduction of slaves into South Carolina from any part of the United States.

In 1803, an act prohibited importation of slaves from the West Indies, and from South America. In 1816, it was enacted that no slave should be brought into the state "from any part of the United

---

2. Ibid., p. 110.
3. Ibid., p. 111.
1. Collins, H. W., *The Domestic Trade of the Southern States*, p. 111.

States or territories or countries bordering thereon." In 1823 and 1847, there were other legislations repealing the law prohibiting the importation of slaves.[2]

Laws were passed in North Carolina restricting the importation of slaves from states in 1786. "A law of 1794 prohibited the introduction of slaves and indentured servants of color."[3] An act of 1776 allowed slaves to be brought in who belonged to residents near the Virginia and South Carolina boundaries. A law, in 1816, was passed providing that slaves brought into North Carolina from foreign countries, contrary to the act of Congress of 1807, were to be sold. No more laws concerning the importation of slaves were passed after the repeal of the laws against importation about 1818.

Georgia in 1793 passed a law against the importation of slaves. In 1798 and 1817, there were other acts concerning the prohibition of the importation of slaves.[1]

A law was passed in 1835 which made anyone subject to fine and imprisonment who should bring into Georgia any male slaves who had been to a non-slave-holding state or to any foreign country.[2] In 1849, all laws civil and criminal forbidding in any manner the restriction of importation of slaves were repealed. Much of the law which had reference to the importation of slaves was repealed in 1852.[3]

Maryland prohibited the importation of slaves in 1783 and 1791 and 1794 were dates of amendment. In the General Assembly of Maryland, it was enacted in 1796[4] that it shall not be lawful, from and after the passing of this act, to import or bring into this state, by land or water, any Negro, mulatto, or other slave, for sale, or to reside within this state; and any person brought into this state as a slave contrary to this act, if a slave before, shall thereupon immediately cease to be the property of the

---

2. Collins, op. cit., p. 116.
3. Ibid., p. 117.
1. Collins, H. W., *The Domestic Trade of the Southern States*, p. 118.
2. Ibid., p. 119.
3. Ibid., p. 120.
4. Ibid., p. 121.

person or persons so importing or bringing such slave within the State, and shall be free.

Immigrants to the state were allowed to bring in their own slaves. In 1797, this was modified in favor of those coming into Maryland to reside. In 1810, a law was passed to prevent those who were slaves for a limited time from being sold out of the state.[1]

A law was passed regulating the exportation of slaves in 1817.[2] A restrictive law was enacted in 1831, which forbade the introduction of slaves into the states.[3] In 1833, the law was withdrawn and supplemented by another act in 1837 which required immigrants to make affidavit declaring their intention to become citizens of the state and to pay a tax on their slaves.

During the years 1776, 1787, and 1793, Delaware and Louisiana made laws restricting the importation of slaves, Delaware being the original southern state to embody a declaration unfavorable to the importation in her constitution.[4]

An Act of Congress in 1798 prohibited the importation of slaves from without the United States. Kentucky, Tennessee, Missouri, Arkansas, Florida and Texas had similar laws from 1790 to 1838, restricting and regulating the importation of Negroes into the states. Although all the states had passed laws to prohibit the introduction of slaves from without the United States before 1808, each state had the power to reopen the slave trade at will.

Congress, exercising its constitutional right in 1807, prohibited the importation of slaves from without the United States after January 1, 1808 and the right of the individual states, to import slaves from foreign states was lost.

4. Fugitive Laws.

Congress passed the Fugitive Slave Bill in 1850. Before the enactment of this bill, a slave could escape from the South and find shelter and refuge in the North. The bill denied the privilege of a

---

1. Collins, op. cit., p. 121.
2. Ibid., p. 122.
3. Ibid., p. 123.
4. Ibid., p. 125.

jury trial, and the escaped slave could be tracked, claimed, and sent back to his owner. The section of the Constitution which declared that no person shall be deprived of life, liberty or property without due process of law or the Habeas Corpus Act did not apply to the slave as he was stripped of every right and reduced to the status of an animal. Under this law, women who had been free were sent back into slavery in many instances.

"Marshals and deputies are required to execute all warrants and precepts, or other process for the arrest and detention of fugitives, under penalty of a fine of a thousand dollars, for the use of the claimant of such fugitive; and in case of the escape of such fugitive from the custody of a marshal, whether with or without his knowledge and connivance, the said marshal is to be liable to a prosecution for the full value of the said fugitive."[1]

"Any person who shall knowingly hinder the arrest of a fugitive, or attempt to rescue him after arrest, or assist such fugitive, directly or indirectly to escape, or harbour or conceal him, shall be liable to a fine of one thousand dollars, and six months imprisonment, by conviction before the proper district or territorial courts, and to a suit for damages of one thousand dollars for each fugitive lost to his owner by said obstruction or rescue, the same to be recovered by action of debt in any of the courts aforesaid."[1]

Rachel Parker, a Negro woman, was taken from her home in West Hottingham, Pennsylvania by a Mr. Schoolfield, a lottery dealer of Baltimore and an agent of M'Creary, a slave-taker. J. C. Miller, with whom the young woman lived, followed in pursuit, and had M'Creary arrested on the charge of kidnapping. Mr. Miller's statement to the effect that he had known the young woman since infancy, and that she was not a slave, resulted in the woman's commitment to the city prison, and Miller and M'Creary were held for appearance in court for the sum of three hundred dollars. When the friends of Miller and of the woman had returned home from the pursuit, Miller was missing. Upon investigation, he

---

1. *The Fugitive Slave Bill and Its Effects*, p. 3.
1. *The Fugitive Slave Bill and Its Effects*, p. 3.

was found dead suspended to a sapling, and although an inquest was held and a verdict of "Death by Suicide" was given, the appearance of his wrists showed that they had been handcuffed and Miller had been murdered.[2]

Amanda Smith, in her autobiography, tells how her father assisted runaway slaves. She states, "Our house was one of the stations of the underground railway. My father took the *Baltimore Weekly Sun* newspaper, which always had advertisements of runaway slaves. These would be directed by their friends to our house, and we would assist them on their way to liberty. . . . at midnight and walk to a place of security, sometimes a mother and child, sometimes a man and wife, and then get home just before day . . . . .[1]

Another story of a slave who escaped is that of William and Ellen Craft who were slaves in Georgia. Since Ellen was fair, she passed as a white woman, and William, her husband, as a slave. With their clever disguise, Ellen as a young planter with a face muffled up from "suffering toothache," and her right arm in a sling, they affected an escape to Philadelphia, stopping on route at the best hotels in Charlestown, Richmond and Baltimore. They were sent to Boston where they lived until the fugitive slave law was passed, and then they went to Great Britain.[2]

It was the duty of the army "to catch run-away slaves"; they were arrested and held subject to the order of their masters. Congress passed an act on August 6, 1861 to confiscate property used for "Insurrectionary Purposes."[3]

Any person, bond or free, convicted of hiding a fugitive charged with crime, was liable to punishment.[4] If a slave, corporal punishment not extending to the loss of life or limb was given; if a free person, a fine of thirty shillings for the first day, and three shillings for each additional day was imposed.

---

2. Ibid., p. 7.
1. Nichols, J. S., and Grogman, U. H., *The New Progress of a Race,* p. 102.
2. Ibid., pp. 103–104.
3. Williams, G. W., *Hist. of the Negro Race in America,* II, p. 263.
4. Flanders, *Plantation Slavery in Georgia,* p. 28.

5. SLAVES AS PROPERTY.

In the fall of 1619, a Negro woman by the name of Angela, was disembarked on the Virginia coast from a ship called the Treasurer of which the Earl of Warwick was owner. This was the beginning of the Negro woman being classified as property.[1]

According to legal terms, a slave was a thing, a piece of personal property, and the laws recognized and regulated it with rigidity and executed it with severity.[2] Although the objection to the idea of property was the prevailing rule, it was not universal, and the objection was individual. The Quakers were the only people, as a group, who protested against this idea of slaves as property. Holding property in man at first was a terrible thing to the Christian religion, but later it sanctioned the custom, with the excuse that the African was a heathen, and slavery would convert him. "Later, when the injustice of holding a fellow Christian in slavery was apparent, it was affirmed by statute that conversion to or acceptance of Christianity does not presume or effect manumission either in person or posterity."[3]

As with other livestock, the proprietor of the female parent became possessed of her offspring and as the owner of a horse might coerce him into subjection, although the law illegalized cruel treatment, and forbade the destruction of life or limb except when meeting resistance or by mishap in the course of "moderate correction." A fugitive slave, like a runaway dog, was advertised, and reclaimed by his master upon payment for services rendered and expenses incurred.[1]

The two following advertisements indicate the low estimate placed on slaves. "One from the *London Gazette* advertised for Colonel Kirk's runaway black boy upon whose silver collar was the inscription, 'My Lady Bromfield's black in Lincoln Inn Fields' and in the *Westminster* announces that he makes silver padlocks for black's or dogs' collars."[2]

---

1. Dowd, J., *The Negro in American Life*, p. 10.
2. Cromwell, J. W., *The Negro in American History*, p. 5.
3. Cromwell, loc. cit.
1. Phillips, *Life and Labor in the Old South*, p. 162.
2. Cromwell, *The Negro in American History*, p. 7.

About 1776, it was not unusual to see advertisements of slave-property. From the *Independent Chronicle,* October 3, 1776, "To be sold a stout, hearty, likely Negro girl fit either Town or Country. Inquire of Mr. Andrew Cillespie, Dorchester, October 1, 1776."

From the *Fame,* November 28, 1776: "To sell—a hearty, likely Negro Wench about 12 or 13 years of age, has had the Small Pox, can wash, iron, card and spin etc., for no other fault but for want of employ."

Also, in February 27, 1777 in the *Fame* appeared:—"Wanted a Negro girl between 12 and 20 years of age, for which a good price will be given, if she can be recommended."

And lastly, from the *Independent Chronicle* of May 18, 1777:— "To be sold for want of employ, a likely Negro girl, 18 years old, understands all sorts of household business, and can be well recommended."[3]

6. PUNISHMENT FOR OFFENSES.

In 1740, by the North Carolina Act, a fine of seven hundred pounds was imposed for the deliberate murder of a slave by his master, or another white man, three hundred and fifty pounds for killing him under correction or in passion, and one hundred pounds for cruel punishment. It was decided in Mississippi in 1820 that wanton killing of a slave by his master was murder. Thirty years later in Georgia, it was declared that a master had absolute power over a slave. In actual practice, a slave had no legal voice, and no penalty was attached to the murder of a slave by his master, although the owner could recover damages if his slave was killed by someone else.

For petty offenses, severe cruelties were imposed by the South Carolina Code of 1712, but later these were modified, and the punishment for stealing was whipping. A common punishment in Charleston and other places was ten lashes for a minor offense. An official whipper received from his patrons fifteen cents for every ten lashes. If resistance occurred, the punishment was

---

3. Moore, G. H., *Notes on the History of Slavery in Massachusetts,* p. 177.

increased two or three times. The death penalty for a slave was hanging.[1]

Crimes and offenses of grave nature which would not fall under the laws of England, received particular attention. The following crimes were declared felonies without benefit of clergy: willful burning or destroying a stock of rice, corn or other grain; setting fire to tar kilns; barrels of pitch, tar, turpentine, rosin or any commodities manufactured in the province. Death was also the punishment for the stealing of slaves and the administering of poison.[1]

Insurrectionary attempts were also punishable by death. The public treasurer paid a sum, not exceeding fifty pounds, when a slave was executed for a crime. Slave owners were forbidden to shelter criminals for the avoidance of property loss. During the colonial period, no offense was punished by branding, but the code provided for corporal punishment or death.

A work house was established for the custody and punishment of Negroes in Savannah, in the year 1763, in order to avoid the owner of slaves the risk of violating the law by the use of "harsh methods" of punishment.

7. OTHER LAWS.

There grew up a system of laws known as the "black laws,"[2] and in 1846 Maryland denied Negroes the right to testify in cases in which any white person was involved; it permitted, however, the testimony of slaves against free Negroes. The legislature in the Constitution of 1851 was forbidden to pass any law abolishing the relation of master and servant.

In 1851, Delaware prohibited the immigration of free Negroes from any state except Maryland. It also forbade them attendance at camp meetings except for religious worship under the control of whites. A law of 1852 provided that no free Negroes should have the right to vote or "to enjoy any other rights of a freeman other than to hold property or to obtain redress in law or in equity for any injury to his or her person or property."[1]

---

1. Brawley, B., *A Short History of the American Negro*, p. 56.
1. Flanders, R. B., *Plantation Slavery in Georgia*, p. 31.
2. Stephenson, *Race Distinctions in American Law*, pp. 36–39.
1. Stephenson, *Race Distinctions in American Law*, p. [?].

In 1847, Missouri forbade any free Negro admittance into the state; it enacted that no person should keep a school for the instruction of Negroes in reading and writing; it also forbade any religious meetings of Negroes unless a justice of the peace, constable or other officer was present, and it declared that schools and religious meetings for free Negroes, were "unlawful assemblages."

Ohio required colored people to give bonds for good behavior, as a condition of residence. This state excluded them from schools, denied them the rights of testifying in courts of justice when a white man was a party on either side, and subjected them to other unjust and degrading disabilities.

In 1851, Indiana prohibited free Negroes and mulattoes from coming into the state and fined all persons who employed them between five and ten hundred dollars for each offense; these fines were to be devoted to a fund for colonization of Negroes. Intermarriage between the races was prohibited.

It was a misdemeanor for a Negro to come into the state of Illinois in 1853 with the intention of residing there, and such persons who violated the rule were prosecuted and fined or sold in order to pay the fine.

Iowa forbade the entrance of free Negroes in 1851, and provided that free colored persons should not give testimony in cases where a white man was involved.

On the ground that it would be dangerous for Negroes to associate with Indians, since there was the possibility of the formation of hostility against the whites, Oregon in 1849 forbade the entrance of Negroes into the state. First, this state tried to keep the free Negroes out, and then it tried to subject them to various disabilities.

The Civil Rights Bill had the effect of making the free states repeal their "black laws," and allowed Negroes intermarriage with whites, attendance at the same schools, the privilege of sitting on juries and the right of voting. The free Negro was in a distinct class between the slave and the master.

Feeling that the free Negro was a sort of irresponsible person, neither bond nor free, and feeling that he would be likely to spread discontent among the slaves, the southern states were afraid of the free Negroes and when the slaves were emancipated, the South desired their leaving. The Virginia Constitution of 1850 provided that the emancipated slaves who remained more than twelve months in the commonwealth after they had become free, should forfeit their freedom and again be reduced to slavery under such regulations as the law might prescribe. If the freedman remained, he would be reenslaved; if he went to a free state, he might be liable to prosecution for violation of laws against immigration of free Negroes.

A Florida statute of 1865 required that all contracts with persons of color should be in writing, and fully explained to them before two credible witnesses. One copy of the contract was to be kept by the employer, and the other by some judicial officer of the state. Contracts of less than thirty days might be oral. Failure to perform his contract, the Negro was treated as a vagrant. In 1866, the law was applicable to both whites and Negroes.[1]

Contracts between white persons and Negroes, by the law of Kentucky, had to be in writing and attested by some white person.

The master might discharge the servant[2] for wilful disobedience of the lawful order of himself or his agent for habitual negligence or indolence in business, for drunkenness, for gross, immoral or illegal conduct; for want of respect and courtesy to himself, his family, guests or agents or for prolonged absence from the promises or absence on two or more occasions without permission. If the master preferred, he might report the servant to the district judge or magistrate who had power to inflict suitable corporal punishment or impose a fine and remand him to work since the fine would be deducted from the wages if not paid.

A servant had the right to leave his master's service for an insufficient supply of food, and unauthorized battery upon his person or upon a member of his family not committed in the defense of the person, family, guest or an agent of the master; invasion by the master of the conjugal rights of the servants or failure by the master to pay wages when due.

At the end of an apprenticeship, the master must pay fifty dollars to a girl and one hundred dollars to a boy, but if the master

---

1. Stephenson, *Race Distinctions in American Law*, p. 47.
2. Ibid., p. 50.

taught the apprentice to read and write, he was not bound to pay any money.

A Negro girl who had been a slave in Maryland and who had been freed by the Constitution of November 1, 1864, was two days later apprenticed by her mother to her former master.

In the statutes of the colony of Virginia, appears the following: "The appearance of Negro, Indian, and mulatto slaves after nightfall in the street without a lighted candle was forbidden, and none were permitted to absent themselves from a master's plantation without written certificate." This law was published every six months in the county court and in the parish churches. It was hoped by this law to prevent the possibility of servile insurrections.

Stroud's Slave Law indicated the general condition as related to slavery.[1]

First–The master may determine the kind, degree and the time of labor to which the slave shall be subjected.

Second–The master may supply the slave with such food and clothing both as to quantity and to quality as he may think proper or find convenient.

Third–He may exercise his discretion as to the kind of punishment to be administered.

Fourth–All power over the slave may be exercised by himself or another.

Fifth–Slaves have no legal rights of property in things real or personal; whatever they acquire belongs, in point of law, to the master.

Sixth–Being a personal chattel, the slave is at all times liable to be sold absolutely or mortgaged or leased.

Seventh–He may be sold by process of law for the satisfaction of the debts of a living or a deceased master.

Eighth–He cannot be a party in any judicial tribunal in any species of action against the master.

Since each state had its own slave code, it is difficult to make a general statement about the legal side of slavery.

---

1. Cromwell, *The Negro in American History,* p. 9.

8. FREEMEN.

There were up to 1790 as many as 59,557 free Negroes in the United States; 35,000 of this number lived in the southern states. From 1790 to 1810, the number exceeded that of the slaves, and from 1810 to 1840 the number remained the same, although the Negro population doubled. The free Negroes were given more consideration than the slaves, and they were not bound by the customs and regulations which restricted the slaves. Many masters maintained schools for their mulatto children. Many of the free Negroes owned considerable property, and some of the number owned slaves who cultivated large estates. Marie Bitand, a free Negro woman, purchased slaves in many instances for personal reasons or in some cases for the purpose of making the lot of the slaves easier.[1]

Although the colonies had special enactments protecting slave property and providing codes and tribunals for this element, they recognized the higher status of the free Negroes.[2] The recruits of the free Negroes came from children born of free Negro parents, mulatto children born of free Negro mothers, mulatto children born of white parentage and manumitted slaves. In this population, the offspring of white men by free Negro mothers contributed much to the numbers in this class. Coming from Europe without wives, some white men cohabited with Indian and Negro women. As evidence shows, such mothers wanted to produce children when supported and protected by the fathers; this was especially true in Maryland and Virginia where there were several instances of this kind. Later, lustful white men found it more convenient to purchase slave woman so that they could appease their animal passions.

Free white woman and white women servants also produced mulatto children. Where there were no social distinctions in regards to race, the economic distinction prevailed. Suffering from the same poverty and discrimination as Negro women during the

---

1. Nichols, J. L., *The New Progress of a Race*, pp. 124–127.
2. Woodson, *Free Negro Heads of Families in the United States* in 1830, p. 6.

early colonial days, the white servant woman or the free white woman intermingled with the Negro men were sometimes in a better position to support them than men of their race.

Some of the Negroes first brought to this country were indentured slaves like white persons of that imported class; at the expiration of their term of service, such Negroes took up land and in some instances they hired indentured servants and owned slaves.

Children born of free Negro and Indian parentage had the status of free Negroes. Planters sometimes married white women servants to Negroes in order to transform their children into slaves, but this was a violation of the ancient law that the offspring of a free woman follow the status of the mother.

Some Negroes became free as an indentured servant became free at the end of their term of service, and it was a matter which concerned the master and slave only and no official could interfere. Since this form of manumission was often objected to as a danger, Negroes obtained their freedom by a last will and testament and by deed.

By the law of 1741, the colony tried to prevent what the General Assembly called "that abominable mixture and spurious issue which hereafter increased in this government by white men and women intermarrying with Indians, Negroes or mulattoes." It was enacted that if any man or woman who was free should intermarry with an Indian, Negro, mustee or mulatto man or woman or any person of mixed blood to the third generation, he should by judgment of the country court, forfeit and pay the sum of fifty pounds to be used for the parish. If any white servant woman should, during the time of her servitude, have a child by a Negro, mulatto or Indian, she should be sold by the church wardens of the parish for two years after the time by indenture.

The law also provided that "An English man or man of any other Christian nation who should commit fornication with a Negro or mulatto woman, should be whipped and the woman sold out of the province." Subjects of England and of Scotland were forbidden to contract matrimony with any Negro or mulatto under a penalty imposed on the person joining them in marriage. An owner could not unreasonably deny marriage to his Negro with one of the same race.

In 1725, a prohibitory law was enacted which provided that no minister, pastor or magistrate or other person who according to the laws of that province usually joined people in marriage should upon any pretense join in marriage a Negro with a white person be fined one hundred pounds. Also if any white man or woman should cohabit with any Negro should be put out to service until they came to the age of thirty-one years; and if any free Negro man or woman should intermarry with a white man or woman, such Negro should become a slave during life and should be sold by order of the justice of the quarter sessions of the respective country. If any free Negro man or woman should commit fornication or adultery with any white man or woman, such Negro should be sold as a servant for seven years and the white man or woman should be punished as the law directs in cases of adultery or fornication.

Although these rigid laws were enacted, they seemed to have little effect on the miscegnation of the races. One fifth of the population at Chester County were mulattoes in the year 1780. The law against the amalgamation of races was repealed in Pennsylvania the same year. Mulattoes constituted one third of the Negro population of Pennsylvania in 1860, although at the beginning of 1820 there was a campaign against intermarriage.

The sister of President Madison said: "We southern ladies are complimented with the name of wives; but we are only the mistresses of seraglio."[1] Many mulatto children were added to the free Negro element by Negro women who were prostituted to the purposes of the young white men and overseers. A respectable "Christian lady" in the south was reported to have kept a handsome mulatto female for the use of her genteel son, as a method of deterring him, as she said, "from indiscriminate and vulgar indulgences."

Harriet Martineau discovered a young white man who, on visiting a southern lady, became insanely enamored by her quadroon maid. He sought to buy her, but the owner refused to sell the girl, but in order to effect the purchase, he finally told her owner that

---

1. Woodson, C. G., *Free Negro Heads of Families in the United States in 1830*, p. 16.

he could not live without the quadroon. Consequently the mistress sold the girl to the young man.

Persons who desired to see slavery prolonged saw that miscegnation and especially the general cohabitation of white men with their female slaves introduced a mulatto race whose numbers would become dangerous if the affections of their white parents were permitted to render them free. They also feared that America would become a race of mixed breeds rather than one of a black and white population.

These laws to prevent intermarriage were never intended to prevent miscegenation of the races, but to debase the offspring of the Negroes to a still lower status. They aimed to leave the Negro woman without redress or protection against white men. Although the intermarriage of the races was prohibited in Maryland in 1663 and the law was made more rigid by other acts of 1681 and 1747, the free Negroes could apparently vote and hold office there, for they were not legally deprived of this right until 1810. Then attempts were made to debase the free Negro's status to that of a slave.

Prior to 1700, free Negroes were tried in the same courts in which white men were tried. Sometimes the free Negro was required to pay a higher poll tax than the white man, and although the free Negroes were not allowed all the privileges of the whites, they were hold liable to carry their part of the burden of the state.[1] There were some exceptions in this case, as it happened that in 1769 free Negro, mulatto and Indian women and all wives other than slaves of free Negroes, mulattoes and Indians were exempt in Virginia.

Most of the social contact of the free Negroes was with the slaves. There was not much difference in the status of the slave and that of the free Negro and many times the two worked side by side. The free Negroes, as a whole, were badly treated.

Negro free men owned and sold their Negro women slaves. Richard Richardson sold to Alexander Hunter in Savannah, a slave woman and child for the sum of eight hundred dollars.

---

1. Woodson, C. G., *Free Negro Heads of Families in the United States in 1830*, p. 32.

Likewise, Anthony Orudingsell, a free Negro, sold a slave woman in the same city in 1833. A Charlestown Negro who purchased his wife for seven hundred dollars sold her at a profit of fifty dollars because she misbehaved.[2]

Marie Louise Bitand, a free Negro woman of New Orleans, purchased slaves for personal reasons in 1832. Samuel Martin, a free Negro slaveholder of Port Gibson, Mississippi, purchased his freedom in 1829, and afterwards bought the freedom of two mulatto women with their four children. He brought them to Cincinnati in 1844 and emancipated them.

Martin Rogues of St. Landry died in 1848 and left a Negro wife with children as well as 4,500 arpents of land, 189 slaves and personal property which was worth forty-six thousand dollars.

Sometimes it was necessary for Negro men to depend upon their wives for support since they could find employment more easily as washerwomen and as seamstresses. One Negro woman who was a slave until the age thirty has property worth two thousand dollars and two houses on which a white lawyer gave her a mortgage of two thousand dollars.[1]

9. EMANCIPATION PROCLAMATION.

The public conscience was quickened and the feeling against slavery was crystallized to such a degree that public men were outspoken against it; societies were organized and the work of the abolition of slavery was begun. A powerful influence was exerted by the principle in the Declaration of Independence that "All men are created equal and endowed by the Creator with certain inalienable rights among which are life, liberty and the pursuit of happiness."[2]

The Colony of Vermont adopted a constitution in 1777 abolishing slavery.[3] Massachusetts framed a constitution in 1780 which contained a provision construed by the courts providing for the abolition of slavery, while Pennsylvania in the same year provided

---

2. Ibid., p. 35.
1. Woodson, C. G., *Free Negro Heads of Families in the United States,* p. 39.
2. Brawley, B., *A Short History of the American Negro,* p. 102.
3. Cromwell, J. W., *The Negro in American History,* p. 10.

for gradual emancipation, though the last slave in this common-wealth did not die until the middle of the nineteenth century.

Rhode Island and Connecticut passed gradual abolition laws in 1784. New Hamsphire followed Massachusetts in 1783 in abolishing slavery. Now five of the original thirteen colonies, prior to the Constitutional Convention of 1787, declared themselves free states, and to which were added New York and New Jersey in 1799, and 1780 respectively. "In the Continental Congress, March 1, 1784, Jefferson proposed a draft ordinance for the government of the Territory of Tennessee, Alabama and Mississippi ceded already or to be coded by individual states to the United States," that after the year 1800 there should be neither slavery nor involuntary servitude in any of the otherwise than in punishment of crime.

This provision was lost to the opposition of the planting interests led by the states of South Carolina and Georgia. The ordinance of 1787 prohibited slavery in the territory north of Ohio which now includes the states of Michigan, Wisconsin, Ohio, Indiana, and Illinois.

In many colonies, the emancipation of the slave was possible only in meritorious cases where a permission from a governor had to be issued. As an illustration of this we have the case of "Will" who was emancipated by the General Assembly of Virginia because he had been signally serviceable in discovering a conspiracy of divers Negroes in in the county of Surry for levying war on the colony of Virginia. He was the slave of Elizabeth, the widow of Benjamin Harrison. "The similarity of the name to that of one of the signers of the Declaration of Independence, the father of one of the presidents and the great grandfather of another, is at least suggestive."[1]

Emancipation was carefully guarded, and the theft of a slave was a capital offense and punishable by death. "The master or his agent was not guilty of a felony should a slave, while resisting his master . . . . . meet with death."[2]

---

1. Cromwell, J. W., *The Negro in American History*, p. 7.
2. Cromwell, J. W., loc. cit.

In a letter to Mr. Horace Greeley on August 22, 1862, Abraham Lincoln wrote: "If there be those who would not save the Union unless they could at the same time save slavery, I do not agree with them. If there be those who would not save the Union unless they could at the same time destroy slavery, I do not agree with them. My paramount object is to save the Union, and not either to save or destroy slavery. If I could save the Union without freeing any slave, I would do it; if I could save it by freeing all the slaves, I would do it; and if I could do it by freeing some and leaving others alone, I would also do that. What I do about slavery and the colored race, I do because I believe it helps to save this Union; and what I forbear because I do not believe it would help to save the Union."[3]

The Union army had won but few victories; fall of 1862 had come and nothing had been accomplished. The president was besieged with requests in the form of addresses, letters and memorials to "do something." A delegation representing the various Protestant denominations of Chicago called upon the President and urged him to adopt a vigorous policy of emancipation as the only method of saving the Union. President Lincoln denied the request.

The delegation, not discouraged, urged that the policy of emancipation would strengthen the cause of the Union in Europe. Nine days after his refusal—September 22, 1862, the President signed the Emancipation Proclamation stating:

"That on the first day of January, in the year of our Lord one thousand eight hundred and sixty-three, all persons held as slaves within any state or designated part of the state, the people where of shall then be in rebellion against the United States shall be then henceforward and forever free; and the Executive Government of the United States, including the military and naval authority thereof, will recognize and maintain the freedom of such persons and will do no act or acts to repress such persons, or any of them, in any efforts they make for their actual freedom."

---

3. Williams, G. W., *History of the Negro Race in America*, p. 254.

Even this proclamation left slaves in many sections since it was only a war measure to save the Union and not a humanitarian measure to free the slaves alone.

II. THE SOCIAL STATUS OF THE NEGRO WOMAN

1. MASTER-SLAVE RELATION.

Negro women slaves were generally shown some indulgence for three or four weeks previous to childbirth. At such times their masters refrained from punishing them. If the women did not finish tasks assigned to them or otherwise failed to perform duties, these omissions were met with only a reprimand. Sometimes they were overlooked altogether. Four weeks generally were allowed, after the birth of a child, before a woman was compelled to go into the field again. When time came for her to return to work she took her baby with her. Sometimes, however, infants were cared for by a slave girl or boy while the mothers were at work. When no child could be spared, or when no child was old enough to look after the infants, the mothers, after nursing, laid their babies under a tree or beside a fence and went on to their tasks. Mothers returned at intervals to nurse their babies.

Babies left in this manner were generally not cared for properly and their lives were often endangered. The women were obliged to work from daylight until dark, without regard to age or physical condition. The same labor was required of women and men alike in many instances, such as digging of ditches, clearing of lands, chopping of cord wood and threshing.[1]

The Negro slaves endured much cruelty as is indicated by this narrative related by an old ex-slave woman.[1] "On a plantation in South Carolina, I witnessed a similar case of suffering—an aged woman suffering under an incurable disease, in the same miserably neglected situation (lying in a corner of the hovel with a few filthy

---

1. The Anti-Slavery Examiner of American Slavery.
1. The Anti-Slavery Examiner of American Slavery, p. 24.

rags under her head). The 'owner' of this slave was proverbially kind to her Negroes; so much so that the planters in the neighborhood said she spoiled them, and set a bad example which might produce discontent among surrounding slaves; yet I have seen this woman tremble with rage when her slaves displeased her, and heard her use language to them which could only be expected from an inmate of Bridewell (a prison); and have known her in a gust of passion to send a favorite slave to the workhouse to be severely whipped.

"Another fact occurs to me. A young woman about eighteen stated some circumstances relative to her young master where they were thought derogatory to this character. Whether false or true, I am unable to say; she was threatened with punishment, but perished in affirming that she had only spoken the truth. Finding her incorrigible, it was concluded to send her to the Charleston workhouse, and have her whipped; she pleaded in vain for a commutation of her sentence, not so much because she dreaded the actual suffering, but because her delicate mind shrunk from the shocking exposure of her person to the eyes of brutal and licentious men; she declared to me death would be preferable; but her entreaties were in vain, and as there was no means of escaping but by running away, she resorted to it as a desperate remedy, for her timid nature never could have braved the perils necessarily encountered by fugitive slaves had not her mind been thrown into a state of despair.

"She was apprehended after a few weeks by two slave-catchers in a deserted house, and as it was late in the evening, they concluded to spend the night there. What inhuman treatment she received from them has never been revealed. They tied her with cords to their bodies and supposing they had secured their victim, soon fell into a deep sleep, probably rendered more profound by intoxication and fatigue; but the miserable captive slumbered not; by some means she disengaged herself from her bonds and again fled through the lone wilderness.

"After a few days, she was discovered in a wretched hut which seemed to have been long uninhabited; she was speechless, a raging fever consumed her vitals and when a physician saw her, he said she was dying of a disease brought on by over fatigue; her mother was permitted to visit her, but ere she reached her, the damps of death stood upon her brow, and she had only the sad consolation of looking on the death-struck form and convulsive agonies of her child."

Angelina Grimké Weld tells of another slave girl who was sent to the workhouse to be flogged, and who was accordingly stripped naked and whipped, leaving deep gashes on her back large enough to insert one's finger where the flesh had been cut out by the torturing lashes.[1]

Another slave-holder, after flogging a little girl of about thirteen years old, set her on a table with her feet fastened in a pair of stocks. He then locked the door and took out the key. When the door was opened, the little girl was found dead since she had fallen from the table. The owner was not held for murder as the child was "Mr. Owner's" property and if he choose to suffer the loss, no one else could do anything about it.

House servants were fed on what the families left. As their food was often short, they were whipped for the crime of stealing food. On the plantations their food was principally hominy. It was really cracked corn, boiled. In the cities the house servants were generally decently clothed, while some favorites among them were richly dressed, but servants on the plantations had the most haggard and squalid appearances.

One writer expresses hope of better treatment of women slaves in her narrative.[1] "However far gone a community may be in brutality, something of protection may yet be hoped for from its public opinion, if respect for woman survives the general wreck; that is gone, protection perishes; public opinion becomes universal rapine, outrages, once occasional, become habitual; the torture which was before inflicted only by passion, becomes the constant product of a system, and instead of being the index of sudden and fierce impulses, is coolly plied as the permanent means to and end; when women are branded with hot irons on their faces; when iron

---

1. The Anti-Slavery Examiner, p. 53.
1. The Anti-Slavery Examiner, p. 153.

collars with prongs are reverted about their necks; when iron rings are fastened upon their limbs and they are forced to drag after them chains and fetters; when their flesh is torn with whips and mangled with bullets and shot and lacerated with knives; and when those who do such things are regarded in the communty and associated with as 'gentlemen and 'ladies'; to say that the public opinion of such a community is a protection to its victims . . ."

The "Mammy" was one of the most important members of the master's family. She often slept in the room with the white children, and all the family secrets were in her keeping. The tie of affection between her and the children she cared for lasted until death. She was frequently the confidential adviser of the older members of the household. To the younger members she also gave advise and to the young mothers, she was an authority on babies; she was regarded highly by whites and blacks. Mammy's cabin was the white children's playhouse, and her authority was next to that of the mistress; her regime extended through two generations, and sometimes three. When the children grew and went away, they embraced her with the same affection as in childhood. At a certain wedding of one of "mammy's" children, she sat like a silent spectre, beside the altar. She was the nurse and foster mother of the bride and could not bear parting with her child.[1]

In a social system constituted of two classes, one exploiting the other, the virtue of women of the subjected class is never respected. American slavery almost universally debauched slave women. If their master approached their chastity, they dared neither to resist nor complain. "A white woman could assume the attitude of self-defence, and if she wounded, maimed, or even killed her brutal assailant, the law would exculpate her, and she would be honored for her resistance; but she who has a colored skin dares not resist or attempt any opposition; and if through the impulse of desperation she would inflict a wound upon her ravisher in the very attempt, she would forfeit her mortal existence if the fact was presented to one of their execrable criminal courts; and if that

---

1. Calhoun, *Social History of the American Family*, p. 283.

course was not adopted her whole life would be subjected of her despot's unceasing and malicious revenge."[1]

Early in the nineteenth century, the North Carolina Supreme Court decided that a white man could not be convicted of fornication and adultery with a slave woman because she had no standing in court. Often in order to produce mulatto girls, masters compelled the slave woman to submit to impregnation of whites, and if they refused, they were punished brutally. Negro women were submitted to every kind of insult. Negro men were exasperated at the deprivation of their wives, but they were helpless in defense of themselves.

This situation of Negro mistresses and white masters caused white women sometimes to be jealous of their rivals. One mistress, on ungrounded jealousy, had slaves hold a Negro girl down while she cut off the fore part of the victim's feet. The girl was then thrown into the woods to perish. A man saved her and her master freed her in order to enable her to escape from the resentment of his wife who did her utmost to get the girl in her power again.[1]

One New Orleans lawyer had a mistress for seven years who was a pretty mulatto girl, while all the time he was courting a white woman. When he married, his wife required that he discard her mulatto rival, and the girl became insane. Another man, who by many years of slave trade from Virginia to Mississippi and Louisiana had made enough money for a good social standing, decided to marry. He had for years kept a beautiful mulatto woman in a richly furnished house with servants to wait on her. The woman was of the belief that she was free, and that her children would inherit their father's wealth. One night she was awakened from her slumber, gagged, and put aboard a steamboat. She was carried away and sold.

2. FAMILY RELATIONS.

The Negro family sprang from two sources. First, family tradition was built up by a large class of free Negroes who had acquired

---

1. Bourne, G., *Slavery Illustrated*, p. 47.
1. Calhoun, A. W., *A Social History of the American Family*, p. 309.

some degree of culture and property; second, the Negro family took roots within the slave institution and grew out of the natural bond of affection existing between man and wife and between parents and children. In instances where slavery took on a patriarchal aspect, the interest of the master often kept them from breaking up families, and some regulation of sex matters were enforced. On the other hand, where slavery was only an instrument of production and subject to the will of the overseer, Negro family ties were broken whenever a matter of economic interest was concerned. When masters were more considerate, slaves had their family in the slave quarters of the plantation.[2]

Marriage systems among slaves were chaotic in its attempt to adjust the African system of polygamy, which deeply involved the structure of the tribe, which was lacking in the new environment to which they were brought. Christian marriage was not introduced to the slaves until the last years of the slave era by missionaries. Slavery was inherited from the mother. The child born of a slave mother took on the status of the mother, irrespective of that of the father. In the female family, the children inherited the mother's status, and property from the mother; descent was traced only through the females.

When white men mated with Negro women, their children were colored and were slaves if the mothers were slaves. A slave woman or a free Negro woman would reside in a white man's house, nominally as a servant or "housekeeper," but actually as a quasi-wife. Although she was not treated as an equal, she assumed the status of mistress of the household. Records show where the masters often bought their housekeepers outright and later freed them. Women received better treatment in this connection than by belonging to the "big house," and often these quasi-marriages were permanent, although not legal. "White men avoided legal marriage with Negro women only because of racial pride."[1] A white wife, in 1830, was more truly a slave in many instances than was her Negro servant, The Negro woman who assumed the posi-

---

2. Frazier, E. F., *The Negro Family*, The Annals of the American Academy of Political and Social Science, Vol. 140, no. 229, Jan. 1928, p. 45.

1. *The Sociological Review*, Vol. 27, no. 1., Jan. 1935, p. 45.

tion of mistress of a home escaped both servitudes, that of wife and that of slave. Large fortunes were also built up by Negro women who had acquired gifts and property from their masters; these fortunes were bequeathed to the children.

A historian of Mississippi pictures the master of the plantation as the head of a family of which the slaves considered themselves members, while the mistress was pictured as head nurse and stewardess since she had charge of the sick, the children and the distribution of clothing.[1]

On some plantations, pregnancy, childbirth and the care of children were matters of great concern. "Pregnant women are always to do some work up to the time of their confinement, if it is only walking into the field, and staying there. If they are sick, they are to go to the hospital and stay there until it is pretty certain time is near."[2] Lying-in women were attended by a midwife and another woman who nursed them for two weeks. Nursing mothers were not required to leave their homes until sunrise, then they left their children with someone. The period of nursing was twelve months. It was a rule that the mother was to cool off, and wait at least fifteen minutes in the summer, before nursing her offspring. At each nursing, the mother was given forty-five minutes to stay with her child. Until the child was eight months old, the mother was allowed to nurse it three times a day: in the middle of the forenoon, at noon, and in the middle of the afternoon. When the child reached the age of eight months, she returned twice a day, missing noon, and at twelve months of age, the mother nursed it at noon only. The nursing mother was supposed to do three-fifths of the work done by a slave. Pregnant women at five months were placed in the suckler's gang, and they were not required to plow or lift heavy objects. Sucklers, old and infirm women received the same allowances as the full work hands. Each woman on confinement was given clothing for the infant, pieces of cloth and food as sugar, rice and flour.[1]

---

1. Calhoun, A. W., *A Social History of the American Family*, Vol. 2, p. 281.
2. Phillips, U. B., *The American Negro in Slavery*, p. 264.
1. Phillips, U. B., *The American Negro in Slavery*, p. 264.

The following marriage ceremony was formulated in Andover, Massachusetts by the Rev. Samuel Phillips after 1710.[2]

"You, Bob, do now in ye Presence of God and these witnesses, Take Sally to be your wife, Promising that so far as shall be consistent with ye Relation which you now Sustain as a servant, you will Perform ye part of a Husband towards her: and in particular, as you shall have ye opportunity and ability, you will take proper care of her in Sickness and Health in Prosperity and Adversity,

"And that you will be True and Faithful to her, and Cleave to her only so long as God, in his Providence, shall continue you and her abode in Such Place (or Places) as that you can conveniently come together.

Do you thus Promise?

"You, Sally, do now, in ye Presence of God, and these Witnesses, Take Bob to be your Husband;

"Promising, that you will Perform the Part of a wife toward him; and in particular, You Promise that you Love him; and that as you shall have the Opportunity and Ability, you will take a proper care of him in Sickness and Health; in Prosperity "And you will cleave to him only, so long as God, in his Providence, shall continue his and your Abode together.—Do you thus Promise? I then, agreeable to your Request and with ye Consent of your Masters and Mistresses, do Declare that you have License given you to be conversant and familiar together as Husband and Wife, so long as God shall continue your Places of Abode as aforesaid; and so long as you Shall behave yourselves as it become the servant to doe:

"For you must both of you bear in mind that you remain still, as really and truly as ever, your Master's Property, and therefore it will be justly expected, both God and Man, that you behave and conduct yourselves as Obedient and faithful Servants towards your respective Masters and Mistresses for the Time being . . . . ."

---

2. Williams, G. W., *History of the Negro Race in America,* Vol. 1, p. 192.

3. PERSONAL NARRATIVES.

If the reader has not already arrived at some conclusion, as to what the social status of the Negro woman was during slavery from the material already given, I feel that citing some of the stories told by slave women themselves will do much to establish a fair idea of her social position during that period.

Harriet Tubman writes:[1] "I grew up like a neglected weed,— ignorant of liberty, having no experience of it. Then I was not happy or contented; every time I saw a white man I was afraid of being carried away. I had two sisters carried away in a chain-gang, one of them left two children. We were always uneasy. Now I've been free, I know what a dreadful condition slavery is. I have no opportunity to see my friends in my native land. We would rather stay in our native land, if we could be as free there as we are here. I think slavery is the next thing to hell. If a person would send another into bondage, he would, it appears to me, be bad enough to send him into hell, if he could."

The woman who gave the following narrative withheld her name for private reasons.[1] "I was held as a slave in—, without even legal right according to the slave laws. When I was ten years old, a young man was punishing me—I resisted; I was in consequence called 'a rebellious wretch', and put out of the family. At the place where I was hired, it happened on communion Sunday in March, that the dogs got hold of a pig, and bit a piece off its ear. In consequence of this misfortune to the pig, a boy of sixteen years, or the abouts, was whipped in the barn; and a man slave was tied up to a tree with his arms extended and whipped. The blood ran as they whipped him. His wife had to take care of him and dress his wounds. It affected me so that I cried, and said I wouldn't stay at the place,—then the same . . . whipped me. At 12 o'clock that night, I ran away . . .

"After my escape from slavery, I married a free colored man. We were comfortably settled in the States, and were broken up by a fugitive slave law—compelled to leave our home and friends

---

1. Drew, B., *A North-Side View of Slavery*, p. 30.
1. Drew, B., *A North-Side View of Slavery*, p. 31.

and go at later than middle life, into a foreign country among strangers . ."

Mrs. James Seward relates:[1] "The slaves want to get away bad enough. They are not contented with their situation. I am from the eastern shore of Maryland. I never belonged but to one master; he was very bad indeed. I was never sent to school, nor allowed to go to church. They were afraid we would have more sense than they. I have a father, three sisters and a brother. My father is quite an old man, and he is used very badly . . . A sister of mine has been punished by his taking her clothes and locking them up because she used to run when master whipped her. He kept her at work with only what she could pick up to tie on her for decency. He took away her child which had just begun to walk, and gave it to another woman—but she went and got it afterward. My master could not manage to whip my sister when she was strong. He waited until she was confined, and the second week after her confinement he said, 'Now I can handle you, now you are weak.' She ran from him, however, and had to go through water, and was sick in consequence.

"I was beaten at one time over the head by my master until the blood ran from my mouth and nose; then he tied me up in the garret with my hands over my head,—then he brought me down and put me in a little cupboard where I had to sit cramped up, part of the evening, all night, and until between four or five o'clock next day without any food. The cupboard was near a fire and I thought I should suffocate . . ."

Here is a story of a slave whose master was her father and Mrs. Henry Gowens gives her account:[1] "My name in the South was Martha Martin. When I came to the North I took the name of Martha Bentley—Bentley being my mother's name before she was married. My father was my master, Mr. —, who died in 1843. He lived in Georgia, but removed with one set of farm hands to Mississippi. He had one other child by my mother, but it died young. He liberated all the children he had by my mother and one other slave woman, with one exception—that was a daughter

---

1. Drew, B., *A North-Side View of Slavery*, p. 41.
1. Drew, B., *A North-Side View of Slavery*, p. 143.

whom he had educated and put to the milliner's trade. After she had learned the trade, he put her in the business. But he found she had two children by a white man. This so enraged him that he carried her two children back to his farm and put her to work in the field and there he said she was to die. The father of the two children came one day and offered two thousand dollars for the woman and the children, as he wished to marry her. But her father would neither let him have her nor his children. Afterwards he offered three thousand dollars, then five other grown up slaves, for Minerva and the two children; but my master told him he would not, but if he ever set foot on the farm again, he would blow his brains out . . .

"I have known many owners to have two or three colored women for wives and when they got a white wife, keep all. If the slave woman would not comply she would be whipped or else sold to the lowest, meanest fellow he could find . . ."

Here we have the story of Lydia Adams.[2] "I am seventy or eighty years old. I was from Fairfax County, Virginia. I was married and had three children when I left there for Wood County where I lived for twenty years, thence to Missouri, removing with my master's family. One by one they sent four of my children away from me and sent them to the South; and four of my grandchildren all to the South but one. My oldest son, Daniel, then Sarah, all gone. 'Its no use to cry about it', said one of the young women, 'she's got to go.' That's what she said when Esther went away . . .

"I've been waiting to be free ever since I was a little child. I said to them I didn't believe God even meant me to be a slave if my skin was black—at any rate, not all my lifetime; why not have it as in old times, seven years a servant? Master would say, 'No, you were made to wait on white people.'

And lastly, Mrs. Sarah Jackson tells her story:[1] —"I belonged to a bachelor, who said I might come away with my three children if I chose. I always desired to come to a free state; and I could not bear the idea of my children being slaves. He did no think I really would leave, although he said I might. There was some opposition

---

2. Ibid., p. 338.
1. Drew, B., *A North-Side View of Slavery*, p. [?].

from his relatives they told me that they thought I was mighty foolish to come away from a good master. I thought I wasn't foolish, considering I had served all my days, and did not feel safe at night: not knowing who I might belong to in the morning. It is a great heaviness on a person's mind to be a slave. I never looked right to see people taken and chained in a gang to be driven off. I never could bear to see my color all fastened together, to go to such a place as down the river. I used to go in the house and shut myself up. I did not know how long before it would be my own fate. I had just enough to pay my way here. I expect to work for a living, and I am trying to get a house. I am better here than I was at home,—I feel lighter,—the dread is gone. I have a sister and brother, slaves in Kentucky. I intend to send my children to school. I have been here about a week."

These personal narratives of slave women serve to indicate in part some of the cruelties, inhuman treatment, rudness, ignorance, poverty and neglect to which the Negro woman was subjected during slavery.

III. THE RELIGIOUS STATUS OF THE NEGRO WOMAN

1. RELIGIOUS BACKGROUND.

The religion of Africans was a belief in a world of spirits and an effort to be guided by them.[1] They believed in the immortality of man and that he could commune with the spirits of the dead. A native placed offerings of food and drink on the grave, and addressed the spirit of the departed. For the natives, there were spirits in the trees, in the birds, and these were spirits of the love ones who had gone hovering about them. While the native believed in God, there were varying conceptions of Him. Some had the idea that God was a generative and fertilizing force, not confined to human beings, so they offered the first fruits of every spring-sowing, and the firstlings of stock-raising as a sacrificial offering in return for having been begotten by Him. Nearly all

---

1. Woodson, C. G., *The Negro in Our History,* see Chapt. 2.

the prayers ended in a petition for fruitfulness of their fields, the blessings of children in their families and aid in propagation. Running throughout the routine of the life of the African was his religion. In their own groups, the African considered an untruth a sin.

The settlement of the Negro in America brought him in contact with entirely new conditions and situations of life to which it was necessary for him to make adjustments.[2] Being a slave, the Negro was exposed to religious domination. They were subjected to a religion which insisted upon obedience to their masters and to their mistresses and which inculcated forgiveness of injuries. It was profitable to the slave holders to teach this type of religion, humility, obedience, and patience, which taught the slave, if he was smitten on one cheek, to turn the other to be smitten also, and that servility was itself a Christian virtue.

A few of the slaves who were brought to America were Mohammedans and a few could read the Koran.[1] The majority of them were uneducated and superstitious. Since in the United States it was a crime to teach the slaves to read and write, they remained illiterate.

Notwithstanding the obstacles the Catholic schools in Washington and Baltimore experienced, they began educating Negro children as early as 1829 but they were compelled to suspend the slave schools as a passage of a law made it criminal to teach a slave to read and write.[2]

2. RELIGIOUS TRAINING.

The religious institutions of the colonies attempted in many instances to convert the Negroes to Christianity, but their efforts were not forceful enough all of the time. Practically every denomination existing in the white institutions was found in the Negro institutions with creeds, rituals, ceremonies. The Negro spirituals of the revival and camp meeting of the nineteenth century were patterned on the words and melodies of the white spirituals.

---

2. Mays and Nicholson, *The Negro's Church*, p. 1.
1. Brawley op. cit., p. 54.
2. *Journal of Negro History*, Vol. 2, April 1917, no. 2, p. 404.

Although the Negroes introduced some changes especially in rhythm, the structure was essentially the same.[3]

"It is easy to suppose that Negroes would have produced a highly emotional type of religious behavior even if the white revival movement had not touched them. It is very doubtful if such would have been the case, however, for in those localities along the seaboard the revival, the prevailing Negro religious behavior is temperate. It is true that in certain isolated sections, like the sea islands of South Carolina, there are probably African elements in the institution known as the 'shout,' but it is interesting to note that the 'shout' is usually segregated from the church service proper."[1]

As a slave, the Negro was considered less than human, incapable of mental discipline through formal training. All rights of citizenship were denied him, and he had to worship and serve God under supervision and close scrutiny. Under this religious domination, the creation of the spirituals was imperative in order that the slave might adjust himself to his new and hostile environment. These spirituals were songs that expressed the restrictions and the dominations which the slaves experienced on the plantation, and the songs represented the soul life of the creators; the following are examples:–

> O Mary, don't you mourn,
> O Mary, don't you weep, don't you mourn;
> > Pharoh's army got drown-ded,
> > O Mary, don't you weep!

> The way of evil doing is wide and fair,
> And many, many, many they do perish there;

> > Pharoh's army got drown-ded,
> > O Mary, don't you weep![2]

---

3. "Social Forces," Vol. 13, no. 1. Oct 1934. *Negro Institutions* – G. B. Johnson.

1. *Social Forces*, Vol. 13–no. 1.

2. See White, N. I., *American Negro Folk Songs*.

> There was a mighty man who came on earth to save,
> Thro' Him we stem the tide of tribulations wave;

> Pharoh's army got drown-ded,
> O Mary, don't you weep!

And this song which one can almost see a Negro slave woman singing:

> Hold my bonnet and hold my shawl
> While I shout in the cool, good Lawd.[1]

The religious songs of the Negroes were not so striking as the songs which their fathers brought from Africa. In singing these songs the slaves would keep time with their feet, or clap their hands, often shedding tears in the rapture of their devotion. There was hardly a plantation in the South where one could not find two or three different sects of christians.

The slaves who were christians were distributed as follows:[2]

Missionary and Hard Shell Baptists	175,000
Connected with Methodist Church South	200,000
Methodist Church North in Virginia and Maryland	15,000
Old School Presbyterians	15,000
New School Presbyterians	20,000
Protestant Episcopalian	7,000
Disciples of Christ	10,000
All other sects combined	20,000

Without regard to differences in religious beliefs, the slaves often held common prayer meetings two nights in every week, where the master sometimes expounded to them the word of God.[3] The slaves managed to weave into their songs the simple picture of the Cross from the tangled threads of their own fancies.

---

1. See Whitem, N. I., *American Negro Folk Songs.*
2. Hundley, D. R., *Social Relations in Our Southern States*, p. 297.
3. Ibid., pp. 348–349.

Their idea of hell was that the Devil was a black man, with horns who literally burned up the wicked with fire and brimstone. Their idea of heaven was that God was a gracious white man presiding over the New Jerusalem, where they would be white angels, wearing silver slippers, walking along payments of gold. The reason for this belief was simple. They had been taught to believe that everything sinful was black and every thing righteous was white. They had been given the worst of life while the whites enjoyed the best; hence their belief that the Devil was black and God, white and that in order to enter heaven they would have to transformed into white angels.

A northern writer was deeply interested in some of the prayer meetings of the slaves and he furnishes the following specimen:[2]

"O my heavenly Father," said an old woman, "I am thy child. I know I love thee. Thou art my God, my portion, and nothing else. O my Father, I have no home in this world; my home is very far off. I long to see it. Jesus is there; thou there, Angels, good men are there. I am coming home. I am one day nearer to it."

This prayer indicates the prevailing psychology of the slaves. They having to endure so many hardships in this life were captivated with a glowing vision of a better life after death.

Some of the planters were actively interested in the religious life of their slaves, providing chapels for their meetings.[1] On Sundays, strictly observed as holidays, in some sections, the children of the slaves were usually taught by some member of the master's family, while church members might worship at a neighboring church if services were not held on the plantation. Sometimes missionaries were employed to instruct the slave, to teach him to be a humble and good servant and to be satisfied with the expectation of a happy life in heaven. There was developed in them the master-slave psychology, exemplified in the hymn, "You can take all the world, but give me Jesus." (The slaveholders took all the world including even the slaves themselves as property, leaving the blacks with only their religion.)

[2.] Adams, D. D., *South Side of Slavery*, p. 55.
1. Flanders, R. B., *Plantation Slavery in Georgia*.

An organized group, "The Association for the Religious Instruction of Negroes in Liberty County, Georgia," in 1831 laid down the following rules for religious teachings:[1]

1. To visit no plantation without permission, and when permitted, never without previous notice.

2. To have nothing to do with civil conditions of the Negroes or with their plantations affairs.

3. To hear no tales respecting their owners.

4. To be no party to their quarrels, but cultivate justice impartiality, and universal kindness.

5. To condemn every vice and evil.

6. To preserve the most perfect order at all meetings.

7. to impress the people with the value of religious instruction and to invite their cooperation.

8. To make no attempt to create temporary excitements or to introduce any new plans or measures; but make diligent and prayerful use of the established means of God's appointment.

9. To support, in the fullest manner, the peace and order of society, and to hold up to their respect and obedience all those whom God, in his providence, has placed in authority over them.

10. To notice no slights or unkindness shown to me personally; to dispute with no man about work, but depend upon the power of the truth and upon the Spirit and blessings of God, with long suffering, patience, and perseverance, to overcome opposition and remove prejudices, and ultimately bring all things right.

The planters fearing the abolitionists or the effect of a revival, exercised great care in their attempt to instruct the slaves, and opposed all excitement or any tense display of emotionalism at the meetings.

Charles Colcock, who was considered the great individual religious instructor among the slaves in Georgia, in addition to laboring for their spiritual welfare, visited the sick and taught the catechism to the children.

---

1. Flanders, R. B., *Plantation Slavery*, p. 176 ff.

3. The Attitude of the Church.

The church exploited the class ignorance of the Negro slaves, and upheld erroneous ideas which it taught concerning the social structure of the world. It was interested in perpetuating the belief in saints, angels and devils; it preached, "Slaves, obey your masters," and, "Jesus was born not to free slaves, but in order to make the bad slave a good slave." The church sanctioned slavery by teaching passages from the Bible which carried the master-slave psychology; examples follow:

"If he (the slave) be not obedient, put on more heavy fetters."[1]

"And that servant which knew his Lord's will and prepared not himself, neither did according to his will, shall be beaten with many stripes."[1]

"Slaves must honor, obey and work for your masters" was the teaching of the church to the slaves.

It was the idea of the church that if the slave was converted into the Christian religion that the benevolent people would be solaced for the whole slavery system. Slaves were expected to attend church where they occupied the gallery seats, sometimes on the corner was reserved for them. On the large plantations, it was customary for slaves to have a meeting on Sundays, the law requiring at least one white person to be present.

In 1724, some questionnaires were sent to the clergy for the purpose of finding out the condition of the Negroes in the colony and at the same time to inquire about the condition of the church. The following questions were asked:[2] "Are there any infidels bound or free with your parish and what means are used for their conversion?" The following answers will illustrate the attitude taken by the church on the subject of the improvement of the Negro race.

"No, excepting Negroes and mulattoes. My means for their conversion is preaching and catechising."

---

1. Ecclesiasticus–Chap. 33, verse 28.
1. St. Luke, Chapt. 12, verse 47.
2. West, G. M., *Status of the Negro in Virginia*, p. 63.

St. Paul's Parish Church answered: "I have no Indians in my parish. The Negroes (when their masters desire it) are baptized when they can say the church catechism."

Gibson, the Bishop of London, in 1727, made a powerful appeal to the colonists, in behalf of the religious education of the Negroes. From the beginning, the "Society for the Propagation of the Gospel" was a holder of slaves. The church in Virginia and the separate ministers themselves in some cases were slave-holders. The Church, although attempting to care for the spiritual welfare of the Negro, sanctioned slavery and in many instances were slaveholders.

In Georgia, as a general rule, the Negroes received the gospel from the same preachers and in the same churches with their masters, occupying the galleries or portions of the church assigned to them. In case separate buildings were provided, the Negro congregation was merely an appendage to the white, the pastor conducting separate meetings for them.

Albert Barnes writes:[1] "Not a few church members are slave holders. Compared, indeed, with all the members of the church in the land, or compared with those who are slave-holders who are not members of the church, the number is few; but in the aggregate the number of members of the church, in all the religious denominations, who hold their fellowmen in bondage, is not small . . . It is to be conceded, also, that a portion of these are ministers of the gospel and others who bear important offices, and who sustain important stations in the churches . . . There are those also in the churches who purchase and sell slaves as they do any other property; who buy them that they may avail themselves of their unrequited labor, and who sell them as they do any other property, for the sake of gain. It is to be admitted, also, that there are those who thus hold slaves under the laws which forbid their being taught to read and who comply with those laws; under laws which restrain their religious liberty, and who comply with those laws; under laws which prevent all proper formation of the marriage relation . . .

---

1. Barnes, A., *The Church and Slavery*, p. 12.

"Not a few ministers of the gospel and members of the churches, either apologize for slavery or openly defend it, even as it exists in the United States . . .'

"There are those who defend the system as one authorized by the Bible and as having for its sanction the authority of God: who refer to it as a "patriarchal institution, sustained by the example of the holy men of early times . . .[1]

"There are those in the ministry, and those who are private members of the churches, who, whatever may be their real sentiments, are, from their position, their silence, or their avowed conservatism, classed in public estimation with the apologists for slavery, and whose aid can never be relied on in any efforts for the emancipation for those who are in bondage. . . .

"Large portions of the church are in the midst of slavery. The institutions which surround the church are those which are connected with slavery . . .

On the other hand, the whole society of Friends opposed slavery as did one half of the Methodist Church in the United States and the entire Methodist denomination abroad. All branches of the Scotch Church were against the system. The Presbyterian Church later recognized the evils of slavery and exerted its influence in attempting to abolish it, as did the Quakers.

Rev. H. B. Albott, pastor of the Methodist Episcopal Church at Augusta, Maine, was formerly a counselor of law in Mississippi. In a letter dated April 10, 1854, says[1]:

"I am acquainted with a Baptist preacher in Mississippi who compelled his slaves to labor on the Sabbath and justified himself under the plea that if they were not at work, they would be sporting, and roving about the fields and woods, thereby desecrating the Sabbath more than by laboring under an overseer."

Throughout the south, Sunday instead of being a day of rest, or of worship was occupied mainly in pleasure and sport for the slave-holder and work for the slaves.[2]

---

1. Barnes, A., *The Church and Slavery,* p. 15.
1. Parsons, C. G., *Inside View of Slavery,* p. 256.
2. Ibid., p. 254.

One minister named Rev. "D" owned Nelly, a quadroon, who was a bright sensitive girl of seventeen. He never allowed her to attend church and on Sundays when he was preaching, Nelly had to dust and put his books in order and clean up his room.[3] Rev. Albert Barnes declared that slavery could not live an hour out of the church, if it were not sustained within it.[4]

The colored churches in the South had no pastors, in the proper sense of that term. Sometimes the pastor of the church to which the slave-holders belonged condescended to address the slaves. When the pastors of the white churches addressed the slave audience, they always counselled obedience and submission, otherwise they would not be permitted to speak.

A preacher who was working among slaves in the south wrote a letter to his brother saying, "All attempts to preach the gospel and to do good there by its influence, are utterly futile."[1] He was of the opinion that as long as slavery existed, the prevalence of religion among the people was impossible; and that the little benefit which morality and decorum produced among the slave-drivers was diminishing. In all the slave-holding States, preachers, lay officers, and church members of all denominations were the most infuriated advocates of the various privations and barbarities which were enacted and enforced under the pretended authority of the "southern institutions."

Also, he thought that the southern churches were one vast consociation of hypocrites and sinners. His reason for thinking this was that the churches received for communion the slave-holders, who purchased slaves and forced lewdness, expressly to multiply the bodies and souls of men and women for the human market, and girls sold for their prostitution and breeding.[2]

The Anti-Slavery Society of Boston wrote that Christian women should loudly denounce that code of laws and that unholy

---

3. Ibid., p. 267.
4. Ibid., p. 269.
1. Bourne, *Slavery Illustrated*, p. 118.
2. Ibid., p. 119.
3. Ibid., p. 122.

practice which nullifies the matrimonial covenent.[3] Also, the society stated that the Christian women should insist that the churches excommunicate the slave-holders and that the women of the north should be a great force in the deliverance of their colored sisters in the south, from the contamination of the slave-holders. If they did not assume this attitude they would virtually be approving the debasement and pollution of their sex.

IV. THE ECONOMIC STATUS OF THE NEGRO WOMAN

1. AS A SLAVE.

Importation of Negroes to the United States was for the purpose of labor. By the toil of their hands, the wealth of this great country was made possible.

A slave could own no property unless by sanction of his master, nor could he make a contract without his master's consent.[1] His marriage was really only concubinage in law, though in case of subsequent emancipation, it would become binding. It was not a crime to rape a female slave; merely trespass upon the master's property! The master was not liable for any damage done by a slave, unless at his order; but to the slave himself and to the community, the master was responsible for maintenance throughout life and for needful medical service. A neighbor, or any other person giving aid to slaves, was entitled to be repaid. Slaves themselves, however, could not be parties to suits at law, nor could they give testimony against white persons.

The body of law applicable to Sante Domingo and Louisiana for the Negroes was called le code noir. The law forbade slaves to possess weapons, to beat drums or blow horns in such a way as to convey signals, to strike any white person even in self defense, and to be out of their quarters after curfew. Many other repressive measures were inflicted.

---

1. Phillips, U. B., *Life and Labor in the Old South*, p. 162.

Slave children were a by product of slavery and their volume could hardly be controlled. The cost of keeping them had no relation to their market price, A woman frequently offered for sale was described as "a good breeder," but she brought little more than a barren woman and was not worth so much as a man of her age. Her service, however, was worth far more than her future progeny, and her fruitfulness, as a mother, automatically lessened her ability to work, during the nursing period. On the plantation, husbands and wives were comrades under the authority of the master, who was captain and quarter-master combined, giving orders and distributing rations.

The basic food allowance was a quart of corn meal and a half pound of salt pork a day for each slave, and, proportionably, for the children. This allowance was supplemented with sweet potatoes, field peas, syrup, rice, fruit, and vegetables, as the season might suggest. Clothes were of coarse materials and shoes were to worn only on Sundays and in the winter. A two-room hut was made to accommodate one slave family. Many of the large plantations were equipped with central kitchens and day nurseries, while infirmaries for scheduled visits were not unknown.

In many instances, the women were given special instruction to make them more efficient in their daily routine, and oft times the slaves assumed positions of relative responsibility.

It often happened that the master obliged a slave woman, who had no children by her first husband, after being a year or two together, to take a second and third husband. A fruitful woman was very much valued by the planters. No slave was allowed to cohabit with two or more wives or husbands at the same time. Babies were more welcome to slave women, sometimes, than to free women, for child-bearing brought lightened work during pregnancy and the nursing period.

The institution of slavery facilitated concubinage not merely by making Negro women subject to white men, but by promoting intimacy and weakening the socalled racial antipathy. Whatever shade or paternity, the children were the property of the mother's owner. Many of the mulattoes were freed by their fathers and vested with property.

Owners of slave women put more value on the women who were prolific in their generating qualities than those who did not bear children.[1] Fecundity was at a premium while admixture of white blood tended to improve the stock. About the end of the eighteenth century, in Virginia, an orphan white girl was indentured to a man who died insolvent, leaving her thus in the hands of a creditor. He treated her as a slave, and compelled her to cohabit with a Negro by whom she had several children. For every impregnation of a female slave, a certain planter offered a white man twenty dollars.

The southern plantation was a great trade school where the slaves received instruction in mechanic arts, in agriculture, in cooking, sewing and other domestic occupations. Although this instruction was given for the benefit of the master, the slaves in many instances got a good industrial training which was a great help when emancipation came. Usually, the women worked along side of the men in the different kinds of labor. Domestic industry was a matter of course, and female slaves in Old Virginia wove coarse cloth and fashioned it into suits. Cotton spinning was a home industry.

In 1679, in Maryland, the servants and Negroes after they had worn themselves down the whole day, ground and pounded the grain for their master's and all their families use.[1]

The specialized slaves, in 1791, at Nomimi Hall consisted of eleven carpenters, two joiners, two gardeners . . . and among the women, three housemaids, two seamstresses, a nursemaid, a midwife, a laundress and two spinsters.

Clothing constituted a large item in the expense maintainance of the slave.[2] The material for their clothing was manufactured on the plantation, although great quantities of coarse cotton cloth for dresses for the female slaves was purchased. Each woman was allotted six yards of cloth, and the children in proportion to their size. New blankets were given every second year, one each to a slave and one to every two children. The women were also given one kerchief and a pair of shoes a piece. For a summer dress each person was allowed a suit of homespun cotton, and the seamstresses on the

---

1. Calhoun, A. W., *A Social History of the American Family*, Vol. 2, p. 245.

1. Calhoun, A. W., *A Social History of the American Family*, Vol. 2., p. 230.

2. Flanders, R. B., *Plantation Slavery in Georgia*, p. 159.

plantation made the garments and mended them. The house servants were clothed in better clothes than the field hands; they often made use of the cast off finery of their mistresses.

Many of the slaves enjoyed the opportunities and privileges of the whites because of the lack of enforcement of the law. They were permitted to rent houses in the neighborhood, and were frequently illegal buyers of spirits and liquors; and during the colonial period slave and free Negroes were taxed as polls.

2. AS A FREEMAN.

Free Negroes were not all on the same plane. In time they developed a social distinction which resembled that of the whites. Many of these were in possession of a considerable amount of property, while others who formed a lower class were mechanics and artisans and often found difficulty in making a living, and were many times subjected to financial embarrassment. The "well-to-do" free Negro did not merely consist of persons with large property attachments, but many of them owned slaves themselves and cultivated large estates. In 1860 of 390 slaves, 130 were assessed with taxes. In 1768, the first tax was levied on free Negroes as a separate class. In 1830, the United States Bureau of Census reported 3777 Negro heads of families owning slaves. Most of these had estates in Louisiana, Maryland, North Carolina, South Carolina and Virginia.[1] As has been mentioned in the earlier part of this study, a free Negro woman by the name of Marie Louise Bitand was a woman of wealth who owned slaves for benevolent purposes. In the city of New Orleans, a free Negro woman owned a tavern and several slaves. Another free woman by the name of Marie Metoyer of Natihitoches Parish owned fifty slaves, and an estate of about 2,000 acres. Most of the "well-to-do" free Negroes in the cities belonged to the artisan class and they numbered considerable. Charleston, South Carolina was a center for thrifty free Negroes and early in the nineteenth century, these free Negroes were ranked by some as economically and intellectually superior to any group in the United States.

---

1. Woodson, C. G., *The Negro in Our History,* p. 246.

The Status of the Negro Woman

At Philadelphia in 1713, the Society of Friends maintained a schoolhouse where instruction was given to girls in sewing and other handicrafts. In 1782 this school went under the charge of Anthony Benezet, who left a large sum of money for the instruction of Negro, mulatto, or Indian children in reading, writing, arithmetic and needlework.

The American Convention of Abolition Societies, in 1796, in its address to the "Free Africans and other Free People of Color" in the United States said:[2] "Teach your children useful trades, or to labor with their hands in cultivating the earth. These employments are favorable to health and virtue. In the choice of masters who are to instruct them in the above branches of business, prefer those who will work with them; by this means they will acquire habits of industry, and be better preserved from vice than if they worked alone or under the eye of persons less interested in their welfare."

Martin R. Delany wrote in 1852: "Let our young men and young women prepare themselves for usefulness and business. . . . A people must be a business people and have more to depend upon than mere help in people's houses and hotels before they are either able to support or be capable of properly appreciating the services of professional men among them. This has been one of our great mistakes–we have gone in advance of ourselves . . ."[1]

Here is a story of the life of a free Negro woman, Mrs. Colman Freeman, as related by her. "I am a native of North Carolina. I was born free and lived with my father and mother. My father was a quadroon—my mother a mulatto. My father fought the British in the Revolution. His father volunteered to take his place, and was in the army seven years. He did not get a pension until three years before he died, not knowing that he was entitled to one, until on some abuse upon white men, he went into court, and the lawyer said, 'Will you suffer injustice to be done to this white-headed old man, who has faced the cannon's mouth, fighting for our liberties;

---

2. *The Annals of the American Academy of Political Science,* Vol. 130, no. 229, Nov. 1928, p. 123.

1. *The Annals of the American Academy of Political Science,* Vol. 130, no. 229, Nov. 1928, p. 124.

who has maintained himself and family without draining a penny from the government?'

"When colored persons had their meetings in the groves, white men would stand with their whips where they were coming out, to examine for passes, and those who had passes would go free,—the others would break and run like cattle with hornets after them. I have seen them run into the river. I remember one time I was going with my brother, and saw them at the meeting trying to get away from the patrollers . . .

"I lived in Ohio, ten years, as I was married there, but I would about as lief live in the slave states as in Ohio. In the slave states I had protection sometimes from people that knew me, but none in Ohio. I understand the laws are better in Ohio now than they were then. In the slave states I had no part in the laws; the laws were all against the colored men; they allowed us no schools, nor learning. If we got learning, we stole it. We live here honestly and comfortably. We entertain many poor strangers."[1]

3. As Emancipated.

Emancipation found the Negro in a very poor economic condition. To be sure, emancipation brought to the children of Negro women advantages and opportunities which were denied the mothers, for they were still the products of a vile system of slavery. Consequently they were ignorant and crude mothers. The comforts and delicacies that go to enhance a home were denied the Negro mother, and she still shared the hard field labor of the men, in many instances. Her house which was a crude log cabin had only two rooms with rough furniture, consisting of tables and chairs. The sheets were few and the mattresses were made of cotton, corn shucks or pine straw, while the pillows were filled with home grown feathers. Sometimes the chimneys were built with logs and daubed over with mud.

Daily meals were prepared in simple fashion with corn meal mixed with water and baked on the top of a hoe or griddle. Bacon and salt pork which was thinly sliced was fried crisp. Bread was served hot with molasses made from sugar cane, and hot water

---

1. Drew, B., *A North-Side View of Slavery*, p. 330.

sweetened with molasses was used as a drink. This bill of fare was served three times daily varied with collards or turnip greens boiled with the salt pork or bacon. One chief characteristic of the cooking was that most meals were fried.

Some of the Negro women, however, had acquired superior skill of the South and were hired to fashionable dressmakers. *The Boston Daily Republican* on August 30, 1840, quoted *The Norfolk Herald:*—"For Sale–a colored girl of very superior qualifications. I venture to say that there is not a better seamstress, cutter and fitter of ladies' and children's dresses in Norfolk or elsewhere, or a more fanciful netter of bead-bags, money purses, etc."[1]

In 1860, there were forty-five free Negro laundresses, one hundred twenty-eight mantua makers, sixty-eight seamstresses and six tailors. In industry, there were eleven slave Negro women cooks, one fruiterer, eleven hucksters, six market dealers, sixteen pastry cooks, free Negro women confectioners, one hotel keeper, twenty-four housekeepers and two slave nurses and ten free Negro women nurses. As apprentices, there were seven free Negro women and twenty-eight houseservants.[2]

V. THE EDUCATIONAL STATUS OF THE NEGRO WOMAN

1. EDUCATIONAL TRAINING.

A justification of slavery has been sought in the alleged belief of the inferiority of the slaves while the broad truism of the possibilities of the human mind was confessed in all legislation that sought to prevent slaves from acquiring an education. The slave-holder asserted his belief in the mental inferiority of the Negro, and then he advertised his lack of faith in his assertion by enacting laws making it illegal to teach him because an education would render him less valuable as a slave, and more valuable as a man taking his rightful place in society.

---

1. See Wesley, C. H., *Negro Labor in the United States.*
2. Ibid.

In 1832, an act of Alabama declared that "any person or persons who shall attempt to teach any free person of color, or slave to spell, read, or write shall upon conviction thereof by indictment, be fined in a sum no less than $250, no more than $500."[1]

The mayor of the city of Mobile in 1833 was authorized by an act of the legislature to grant licenses to such persons as they deemed suitable to give instructions to the free colored Creoles.

In Arkansas, there did not appear any laws against educating the Negroes, but an impression was left that Negroes were denied the right to be educated.

There was a strong prejudice against educating the Negroes in Connecticut, although there was no legislation against it.

Delaware never passed any law against the instruction of Negroes, but in 1833 every person was taxed who sold slaves out of the state or brought one into the state, five dollars.

In 1848 in Florida, only white children were allowed school privileges, and In Georgia in 1770, a fine of twenty pounds was inflicted for teaching a slave to read or write.

A penalty of $100 was provided against persons who employed any slave or free person of color to set type or to perform the act of teaching them to read or write. The Illinois schools contained the word white, although there was no prohibition against the education of colored persons. Before the Civil War separate schools were established. No provision at all was made for the education of Negro children in Indiana.

In Kentucky, the property of the colored persons was taxed by an act of 1830, but they were excluded from privileges of schools. By an act of 1830, it was against the law in Louisiana to teach or permit or cause to be taught any slave to read, or write and free Negroes were denied the entrance into the state.

Maine gave school privileges to all citizens without regard to race or color by her Constitution of 1820, but in Maryland there was nothing on the statute book to prohibit the education of

---

1. Williams, G. W., *History of the Negro Race in America*, Vol. 2, pp. 148–196.

Negroes, but the law designated that the schools were for white children.

St. Frances Academy for colored girls was founded in connection with the Oblate Sisters of Providence Convent in Baltimore, June 5, 1829.

A separate school for colored children was established in Boston in 1798, and the first primary school was established in 1820. In 1855, the separate schools were discontinued in accordance with the general law passed by the Legislature which provided that "in determining the qualification of scholars to be admitted into any public school, or any district school in this commonwealth, no distinction shall be made on account of the race, color, or religious opinion of the applicant or scholar."

In Mississippi in 1846 and in 1848, school laws were enacted, but schools and education were prescribed for the white youth between the ages of six and twenty years.

Free Negroes were ordered out of the state of Missouri in 1845 and in 1847 an act was passed providing that "no person shall keep or teach any school for the instruction of Negroes or mulattoes in reading or writing in this state."

A school for Negro slaves was established in New York in 1704. Public schools for Negro children were started in 1832, and in 1852 the first evening schools for colored were opened. In North Carolina, until 1835, free Negroes were allowed to maintain schools. The public school system provided that no descendant from Negro ancestors, to the fourth generation inclusive, should enjoy the benefit thereof.

The first schools for colored children in Ohio were established at Cincinnati in 1820. In 1849 the Legislature passed an act establishing schools for colored children to be maintained at the public expense. Oberlin College allowed colored students to enter from the moment of its existence in 1833.

The first seminary in the District of Columbia for colored girls was established in Georgetown in 1827. The female seminary was under the care of Maria Becroft, who was the most remarkable colored young woman of her time. She was born in 1805 and died in December 1833.

Miss Myrtilla Miner's seminary for colored girls was established at Washington, D. C. Opposition to the school throughout the district was strong. The house in which the school was then housed was set on fire in the spring of 1860, when Miss Miner was asleep in the second story, but the smell of smoke awakened her in time to save the building and herself from the flames. Another school was established in Washington by Mary Wormley in 1830 for colored youth.

The first school for contrabands was started in September 17, 1861 in Hampton by a Negro woman, Mrs. Mary Peake, who was the first of a distinguished line of teachers in the mission schools. Little schools were scattered throughout the "tide water" section, and at the close of the Civil War, the mission school was an important factor in educating the Negro.[1]

The law forbade white men to marry the Negro woman, but despite the law many slave-holders took her as a wife; and when she gave them children, they were cared for and educated. Sometimes they were sent to northern schools, sometimes to France or to England.

2. SPECIAL ACHIEVEMENTS.

This section will contain a short survey of pioneer Negro women, who blazed the trail for the coming generations of Negro women, giving them hope for a better day; and who in spite of all the indignities inflicted by the institution of slavery, and all of the hardships and discriminations they endured, advanced the progress of the race and made their contribution to American civilization.

a. Phillis Wheatley.

Mr. and Mrs. John Wheatley, wealthy New Englanders purchased Phillis at the age of six years at Boston in 1761.[1] As her real name was not known, she was given the name "Wheatley." She was a very precocious child, exceedingly patient and over studious and not over strong. Her ability to learn was extraordinary, and after sixteen months of study, she had mastered the English language

---

1. Merriam, G. S., *The Negro and the Nation,* p. 94.
1. Nancy Cunard, *Negro Anthology.*

and her first poem was written in 1770. This stimulated her ambition which caused her to become well acquainted with grammar, history, geography and astronomy, and she also mastered Latin to the extent that she was able to read Horace with ease and enjoyment. Phillis Wheatley had access to the best libraries in Boston which gave her opportunities to talk with accomplished persons. By her cultural and educational improvement, she shed her position as menial slave, and won the status of companion for Mrs. Wheatley.

In 1772 Phillis, because of failing health, was sent back to England with the Wheatley's son. She was introduced to many of the nobility, and was preparing to receive court when she received a message from America stating the illness of her mistress; this caused Phillis to return immediately.

It was from England in 1773 that her first volume of poems was published under the patronage of the Countess of Huntington and dedicated to her. Some of the people doubted Phillis' authorship of the volume and Mr. John Wheatley wrote a letter signed by prominent citizens affirming the authenticity of her authorship.[1]

It was thus that, "Poems on Various Subjects, Religious and Moral," was given to the literary world; these poems were widely read and enjoyed.

Phillis became a member of the Old South Church in Boston, and under her religious influence, wrote these lines:

> " 'Twas mercy brought me from my Pagan land,
> Taught me benighted soul, to understand,
> That there's a God, that there's a Saviour too.
> Once, I redemption neither sought or knew,
> Some view our sable race with scornful eye,
> Their color is a diabolic dye—
> Remember, Christians, Negroes black as Cain
> Can be refined and join the Angelic train!"[2]

---

1. This reflects the white superiority attitude—that the Negro was incapable of achievements.

2. Cunard, N. *Negro Anthology*, p. 164.

In April 1776, a poem was printed in the *American Monthly Museum* entitled "His Excellency, General George Washington." After that Mr. and Mrs. Wheatley died, leaving Phillis alone and destitute, as the son was still in Europe. She then married a lawyer named Peters. On December 5, 1794, Phillis died.

As an appraisal of her work, it is said that her poetry was remarkable and ranked with the best of American echoes of the English classists, and her prose, which was in the form of letters, was original, amusing and at times sparkling with genius and wit. These letters were published in Massachusetts by the Historical Society in 1863–1864.

Phillis Wheatley was the first of the Negro race to attempt the muses, and one must consider the depths from which she came in appraising her work rather than by the heights to which she rose.

b. Sojourner Truth.

It is thought that Sojourner Truth was born in 1777, but the exact date of her birth is unknown; she died in 1883.[1] Before she was liberated, in 1817, she had served five masters, had been married and had given birth to five children, who were sold away from her in slavery. Because of her wanderings, she changed her name from Isabella to Sojourner, and Truth was added as a name because she felt that God had called her to preach the truth about slavery.

Harriet Beecher Stowe says, "I never knew a person who possessed so much of that subtle, controlling power, called presence, as Sojourner Truth."[2]

Sojourner Truth went to Washington and visited President Lincoln at the White House to plead for the enlistment of Negro men in the army; to this plea Lincoln and Congress later gave their consent. In 1861, there at Washington, she cared for the wounded soldiers, instructed and provided for the homeless emancipated slaves, who were half-naked and half starved.

At the close of the Civil War, Sojourner Truth, who was then ninety years old, travelled and lectured for the freedom of the slaves along with William Lloyd Garrison, Wendell Phillips,

---

1. Cunard, N., *Negro Anthology.*
2. Ibid., p. 175.

Frederick Douglass and others. In 1851, the Suffrage Convention at Okron, Ohio, credited her with having saved the day for the women. "Despite her inability to read or write, she counted among her most cherished possessions a tiny autograph book; among the many extracts, testimonials and names of distinguished persons found therein is the following:—For Aunty Sojourner Truth, A. Lincoln." October 9, 1864.[1]

Sojourner Truth died on November 26, 1883 and was buried in Oakhill cemetery, Battle Creek, Michigan.

c. Harriet Tubman. (1820–1913).

After effecting her own freedom, Harriet Tubman successfully made thirteen perilous trips back and forth over the underground railway to conduct four hundred slaves to their freedom, and although $12,000 was offered as a reward for the "black shadow," she escaped.

Harriet Tubman with this great Underground Railroad system directed defiance to the omnipotent Fugitive Slave Laws of 1850. Various routes were used and "General Moses", as Harriet Tubman was sometimes called, was a woman of extraordinary endurance and strength. She had no equal in the point of view of courage and wit in rescuing her fellowman. The first twenty-five years of her life was spent as a slave on a Maryland plantation.

The routes in the "Underground Railroad" were known as "lines," stopping places were called "stations," and those who aided along the way were called "conductors," and their charges were known as "packages" or "freight." The system was an elaborate network which reached from Kentucky to Virginia, across Ohio, and from Maryland, across Pennsylvania and New York. The Quakers aided from 40,000 to 100,000 slaves to freedom.

At the age of six, Harriet's master injured her skull with an iron weight, and the injury resulted in pressure on the brain, which caused her to fall asleep at most any time. In spite of this unfortunate physical handicap, her followers had implicit faith in her and her slogan was, "A live runaway slave can do great harm by going back, but a dead one can tell no tales."

---

1. Cunard, N., *Negro Anthology,* p. 181.

Harriet Tubman displayed strength of character rarely possessed by one in any station of life, and her name belongs along side of Joan of Are and Florence Nightingale. She had patience, foresight, loyalty, tenacity and sagacity. It is said that her last words were to the Association of Colored Women, "Tell the women to stick together; God is fighting for them, and all is well."

The city of Auburn, New York bears a silent testimony in honor of Harriet Tubman on one of its public buildings; in Boston there is a settlement house named after her. Harriet Tubman was born of Harriet Ross, her mother, the daughter of a white man, an American, and her father was a full-blooded Negro.

d. Catherine Ferguson. (1749?–1854).

Catherine Ferguson is the founder of the First Sunday Movement in the United States and in 1773 in New York City she opened the Katy Ferguson's school for the poor.[1] As the opportunities for an education for the poor were few, this effort of Catherine Ferguson has an important place in the beginnings of education in the United States.

She was an ex-slave and at the age of eight her mother was sold from her. At the age of eighteen, she married and had two children, who later died. In the history of educational achievement, Catherine Ferguson's name should be placed with those of Herbart, Pestalozzi and Horace Mann.

e. Mary Ann Shadd Cary.

Mary Ann Shadd was born on October 9, 1823 in Wilmington, Delaware.[2] She was educated by Phoebe Darlington under the supervision of the Society of Friends; after the completion of a six-year course, she returned to Wilmington and opened a school and taught colored children. Later she taught public school in West Chester, New York and Norristown, Pennsylvania. While teaching in Pennsylvania, in 1858, the Fugitive Slave Act was passed; this made her decide to go to Canada to ascertain what opportunities the country offered for the settlement of emigrants of colored peo-

---

1. Brown, H. Q., *Homespun-Heroines*.
2. Ibid.

ple. To make her work more effective, she returned to the United States and delivered lectures.

In 1854 she established a weekly paper called *The Provincial Freeman*, which was devoted to colored people, especially to fugitives.

Mary Ann Shadd married Thomas F. Cary of Toronto in 1856. At the beginning of the Civil War, Mrs. Cary was teaching in Michigan. On August 15, 1863, she was appointed by special order, Recruiting Army Officer, to enlist colored volunteers in the Union Army. Later she was appointed in the public school system of Washington, D.C., and for seventeen years was principal of three schools.

She also was a regular contributor to the newspapers, *The New National Era*, and *The Advocate*. In 1884, she graduated from the Law Department of Howard University. Mrs. Cary died in Washington, D.C., June 5, 1893.

f. Frances Ellen Watkins Harper (1825–1900).

Frances Ellen Watkins was born in the city of Baltimore, Maryland in 1825, of free parentage. At the age of three years, she lost her mother by death, and she was sent to Rev. William Watkins, an uncle, who taught a school in Baltimore, where she remained for instruction until she was thirteen years of age.

At the age of fourteen, she wrote an article which displayed her literary talent. Later she published a volume called "Autumn Leaves."

In 1850, she was the first Negro woman to do vocational work in Columbus, Ohio at Union Seminary which later became Wilberforce University. Next, she went to Little York to teach and while there witnessed the "Underground Railroad." She visited Philadelphia, New Bedford, and Boston where she attained the position of lecturer on September 28, 1854 for the Anti-Slavery Society of Maine.

Frances Ellen Watkins married Fenton Harper in 1860 in Cincinnati where she continued her literary and anti-slavery activities.

Among the best known of her prose and poetry are "Moses," "A Story of the Nile," "The Dying Bondsman," "Eliza Harris

Crossing the Ice" and a book entitled, "Iola Leroy." Mrs. Harper was the first Negro woman to write a novel.

The vividness of her poetry is evidences in this first stanze from "Eliza Harris."

> Like a fawn from the arrow,
>   startled and wild,
> A woman swept by us, bearing a child;
> In her eye was the night of a settled despair,
> And her brow was o'er shaded with
>   anguish and care.[1]

These are only accounts of a few of the Negro women of that earlier period, who, under the most unsatisfactory and difficult circumstances made achievements that stand out in bold relief.

VI. SUMMARY

Slavery was not recognized by the common law of England. It is true that in the latest reign of Charles II some recognition was given to colonial merchants who sometimes brought slaves to ports in England, and held them there temporarily. After the middle of the seventeenth century, Blackstone wrote in 1760, declaring that the law of England would not endure the existence of slavery. Lord Mansfield decided the "Somerset Case" that the state of slavery was so odious that nothing could support it than that of a positive law.

The charters of the various colonies provided that laws of colonial governors should be as near as convenient, agreeable to laws, statutes and government of the policy of England. This was expressed in the Virginia Charter of 1619. Charters of other colonies substantiated the same effect.

---

1. Watkins, F. E., *Poems on Miscellaneous Subjects*. Printed in Boston by J. B. Yerrington & Son–1854.

This seemed to inhibit slavery in the colonies, but that was only a bridge over which much indigenous law and custom got into colonial law. In thirty years, from 1619 to about 1649, there were three hundred slaves in Virginia.

In Virginia, the original planters were themselves servants, and they sought more servants. In 1618, they petitioned the crown that vagabonds and condemned criminals be sent out as slaves. Political prisoners were sent from England as indentured servants to serve a term of years in this country.

Although 300,000 Negroes were imported into the colonies before the Revolution, not all slaves were Negroes. In early records, Negroes were described as servants, not as slaves. Many were freed at the end of the term of service.

By common law, slavery was not recognized until 1661 by the statute of Virginia. A year later, the status of the child of a slave depended on that of its mother.

The slaves increased to such an extent that the whites became afraid of slavery. From 1726 until the Revolution, almost at every session of the Virginia Assembly, the question of restricting slave trade was debated. Nevertheless, the king issued instructions to the governor showing his highest displeasure to any law that would prohibit the importation of slaves.

There was a feeling of revulsion regarding slavery in the later part of the colonial period. This was attributed to the great revival of religion in the colonies from 1740 onward. This attitude was strengthened by the influence of the French political philosophy with its exaltation of liberty. The religious sects were active in this religious revival and was soon manifested in a strong opposition against slavery by the Congregationalists, Methodists, Baptists and Quakers.

In 1780, Pennsylvania passed laws providing for gradual abolition of slavery, and most of the northern states, including Vermont, adopted similar policies. Massachusetts abolished slavery in one stroke, and the Pennsylvania law abolished slavery a day later. New Hampshire also abolished slavery at one stroke. The Northwest Ordinance of 1787 prohibited slavery in the great northwest territory.

Some of the southern states in the Constitutional Convention objected to any provision that would prohibited importation of slaves and compromises were reached in the convention on many points.

Article 1, Section 9, in the original Constitution provided that migration and importation of such persons as the states now existing shall think proper to admit by the Congress prior to 1798, but it provided that tax or duty imposed on such importation should not exceed ten dollars for each person.

The Fugitive Slave law provided that the slave must be delivered up. At the time of the adoption of the Constitution, five states declared that free Negroes were citizens and enjoyed suffrage. The privilege was removed in North Carolina and New Jersey, which were two of the five states. In most states, free Negroes were not held to be citizens. The passage of the act of prohibition of slave trade in 1808 was advocated by President Jefferson. Thousands of Negroes were smuggled into the country. Promoted by the spirit of the Revolution, many slaves were freed, and as early as 1800, there were a large number of free Negroes which were deemed to be a menace in the south only.

The reaction to this attitude was fostered by the invention of the cotton gin by Eli Whitney. The price of cotton soared and cotton was king. The Dred Scot decision in 1857 declared that free Negroes were not citizens.

The Emancipation Proclamation issued by President Lincoln was an announcement of policy rather than a statement of accomplished fact. It really gave the Negroes a very unsatisfactory legal status and slavery was not really abolished until the adoption of the thirteenth amendment, and the question of Negro citizenship was not settled until the adoption of the fourteenth amendment of the Constitution of the United States.

The Negro woman lived in a world where the white man could work his will on her without hindrance of the law, and she was outside the influence of social codes and the moral restraints which protected the virtues of the white woman. Besides having an extra-legal position in the South, she had an extra-social status which rendered her safe prey for the white man's lust. She was pursued by him for immoral ends without dread of ill consequences to himself either legal or social.

Chattel slavery subjected Negro women to rudeness, ignorance, poverty and neglect. Upon her fell all the direst curses of slavery, its cruelties, violence and lusts. Under this malign spell, her soul was saddened, her heart embittered, and all the instincts of womanhood blurred and enfeebled. Neither exploitation nor lust was spared her; her life was one of long drudgery and suffering as soon as she was old enough to go into the field. She was driven to work at sunrise and at sundown when she returned weary and faint, she had to cook and eat a coarse meal of corn and bacon, then rest, herded with her fellow-slaves in quarters where little distinction was made of sex or age.

Children, whom she bore, were not her own, but only property to be disposed of at will of the slaveholder. The Negro woman's position was one of peril; she was subjected to a double moral standard, one for her and one for her white sister. The Negro woman was not protected by law, nor by public opinion, against the sexual passion and pursuit of the southern white "gentlemen." The South did not realize that in order to maintain a high moral standard that it was essential to elevate the morals of both races. They did not realize that the institution of slavery produced a moral deterioration on both masters and slaves.

At the present time, Negro women in the south are working under a system of semi-slavery and exploitation. They are discriminated against both as Negroes and as women. They get the lowest wages and the least desirable work. To overcome these injustices and inequalities, the Negro women will have to fight in order to get full legal, social, economic and educational equality.

BIBLIOGRAPHY

Barnes, A., *The Church and Slavery*. Philadelphia: Parry and McMillan, 1857.

Brawley, B., *A Short History of the American Negro*. New York: Macmillan Company, 1927.

*Brown, H. Q., *Homespun Heroines and Other Women of Distinction*. Xenia, Ohio: Aldine Publishing Company, 1926.

*Calhoun, A. W., *A Social History of the American Family*. Cleveland, Ohio: The Arthur H. Clark Company, 1917. 2 Vols.

*Collins, W. H., *The Domestic Slave Trade of the Southern States*. New York: Broadway Publishing Company, 1914.

*Cromwell, J. W., *The Negro in American History*. The American Negro Academy, 1914.

*Cunard, Nancy, *Negro Anthology*. London: Weshard and Company, 1934.

Dowd, J., *The Negro in American Life*. New York: New Century Company, 1926.

*Drew, Benjamin, *A North-Side View of Slavery–The Refugee or the Narratives of Fugitive Slaves in Canada Related by Themselves*. Boston: John P. Jenett and Company, 1856.

*Flanders, R. B., *Plantation Slavery in Georgia*. Chapel Hill: The University of North Carolina Press, 1933.

Kelsey, Carl, *The Negro Farmer*. Chicago: Jennings and Pye, 1903.

Kirkland, E. C., *A History of American Economic Life*. New York: P. S. Crofts and Company, 1933.

Mays, B., Nicholson, J. W., *The Negro Church:* New York: Benjamin New York Institute of Social and Religious Research, 1933.

Merriam, G. S., *The Negro and the Nation*. New York: Henry Holt and Company, 1906.

*Moore, G. W., *Notes on the History of Slavery in Massachusetts*. New York: D. Appleton Company, 1866.

*Nicholos, J. L., William, A. B., Grogman, H., *The New Progresso* of a Race. J. L. Nicholas and Company, 1925.

Parrington, V., *Main Currents in American Thought*. New York: Harcourt, Brace and Company, 1927. 2 Vols.

*Phillips, U. B., *Life and Labor in the Old South*. Boston: Little, Brown and Company, 1929.

Phillips, U. S., *American Negro Slavery*. New York: D. Appleton and Company, 1918.

*Poore, *Federal and State Constitutions of the United States*. Washington: Government Printing Press, 1877. 2 Vols.

*Stephenson, G. T., *Race Distinction in American Law*. New York: D. Appleton and Company, 1910.

*Wesley, C. H., *Negro Labor in the United States 1850-1925*. New York: Vanguard Press, 1927.

*West, Gerald M., *The Status of the Negro in Virginia During the Colonial Period*. New York: Jenkins Company, 1897.

White, N. I., *American Negro Folk Songs*. Cambridge: Harvard University Press, 1928.

*Williams, G. W., *History of the Negro Race in America*. New York: G. P. Putnam's Sons, 1883.

*Woodson, C. G., *The Education of the Negro Prior to 1861*. New York: G. P. Putnam's Sons, 1915.

*Woodson, C. G., *The Negro in American History*. Washington, D.C.: Associated Publishers, 1931.

*Woodson, C. G., *Free Negro Heads of Families in the United States in 1830*. Washington, D.C.: The Association for the Study of Negro Life, 1925.

BOUND PERIODICALS

The Anti-Slavery Examiner of American Slavery as It is: Testimony of a Thousand Witnesses. New York: American Anti-Slavery Society. Bound in seven sheets–1839.

PERIODICALS

Cousins M. Winifred, *Slave Family Life*. Sociological Review. Vol. XXVII, No. 1, Jan. 1935.

Johnson, B. Guy, *Some Factors in the Development of Negro Social Institutions in the United States*. The American Journal of Sociology, Vol. XL, No. 3, Nov. 1934.

Frazier, E. F., *The Negro Family*.

Nichols, R. F., *The Progress of the American Negro in Slavery*.

Gregg, E. J., *Industrial Training for the Negro*. The Annals of the American Academy of Political and Social Science, Vol. CXXXX, No. 229, Nov. 1928.

PAMPHLETS

Leed Anti-Slavery Series, No 32.
The Fugitive Slave Bill and Its Effects.

*The books starred were used extensively and a thorough study was made
of them in the preparation of this thesis.

POETRY

April Night

The moon illuminates the April sky
With a white, crystalline, filtering light.
A shrill, piercing wind whistles high
Above the rustling pines, in flight,
And the cool, dripping rain gleams,
Splashing the desolate night with dreams.

I am ravished with your primrose beauty,
The wind-swept sky, lined with immortal hue.
For me you are my frailest dreams come true;
O glorious-tinted June, have pity!

My weary breast is filled with quiet yearning;
Do not deride my poor enraptured heart,
Nor hold me off, nor as a thing apart,
For now all my passion's fire is burning.

You are eternal as a mountain pine;
All day, I kneel below your petalled shrine.

Buried Deep

When I am cold and buried deep away,
And have no zest to live or to return,
Come to my grave and flower-strew the clay,
And dance and sing, but never weep or mourn.

Cradled Gifts

Break down that futile
Wall of cynicism,
And let me fold you
In the trellis
Of my arms;
Let me hold you
In the fortress
Of my breast;
Let me mould you
Cradled gifts
Of love.

Elysium

Beloved, tonight
You and I walk hand in hand,
Over hard, barren ground
In the cool, nebulous darkness.
The dusty, trodden road
Rambles along, dingy and grey
From rains and rotting leaves.
The trees murmur in the breeze
Like the sound of distant violins.
Let us return,
You and I,
To the land of dreams
That once was yours and mine.
Let us return
And quench our thirst
At wells of old forgotten memories.

I See You

I see you
Standing in the garden
With a lily in your hand.
It is drooping
Like the half-moons
Of your eyes.
My love is a rose
I cast at your feet.
Lift it from the earth
That you may inhale
Its delicate fragrance.
It is the essence
Of my soul.

I Understand

I did not understand:
I only knew
That ere he turned to go
His eyes strayed to the Madonna,
There on my chamber wall.
She smiled on the Infant Jesus
Cradled in her arms.
Sorrow wells in this breast
No child has e'er caressed.
From my window, I see
Naked trees, stripped of their leaves.
Now he is gone,
I understand.

Let Your Rays

Let your rays
Beam upon me,
O sun!
Illuminate my soul.
Whirl your waves of heat
Against my breast,
And melt my frozen heart.

Love Me

Love me,
I would command.
But do not decide—
Leave the question open.
Your passional nature
Will not decide now,
On intellectual grounds.
Your passion is stronger
Than your technical rule
To choose
An undetermined truth.
Let logic, later, rule
Your action.
Love me,
I would command.

One Summer's Day

One Summer's day
Love and I
Walked toward the horizon.
The cool, fresh breeze
Played among the trees.
We grew weary,
Love and I,
And fell asleep.
When I awoke
I was alone . . .
Love had gone.

Sonnet for June

With praise of you I bring song and psalter,
I breathe in deep draughts from the fragrant earth,
Which quickens me with ecstasy and mirth;
And all the day, I kneel at your altar.

Tribute

Your graceful bronze limbs
Are like palm leaves
Moving rhythmically
In the wind.

You'd wear your nudity
With charming candor:
The artificial and false
You abhor.

Your body is beautiful
And strong,
Your sensibilities
Fragile,
Your nature artistic.
My dormant soul is stimulated
By your smile.

Worship

A bird carolling
Among the trees—
And dewdrops glittering
On a rod—
A sunbeam quivering
In the breeze—
Rosebuds opening their
Beauty to God.

Young Love

Let my hair hang
Upon my shoulders.
Weave a wreath of jasmine
Into its strands.
Kiss each blossom, and promise
You'll love me always.
Then I'll bind my hair
About my head
And hold your love secure.

ABOUT THE EDITORS

Henry Louis Gates, Jr., is the W. E. B. Du Bois Professor of the Humanities, Chair of the Afro-American Studies Department, and Director of the W. E. B. Du Bois Institute for Afro-American Research at Harvard University. One of the leading scholars of African-American literature and culture, he is the author of *Figures in Black: Words, Signs, and the Racial Self* (1987), *The Signifying Monkey: A Theory of Afro-American Literary Criticism* (1988), *Loose Cannons: Notes on the Culture Wars* (1992), and the memoir *Colored People* (1994).

Jennifer Burton is in the Ph.D. program in English Language and Literature at Harvard University. She is the volume editor of *The Prize Plays and Other One-Acts* in this series. She is a contributor to *The Oxford Companion to African American Literature* and to *Great Lives from History: American Women*. With her mother and sister she coauthored two one-act plays, *Rita's Haircut* and *Litany of the Clothes*. Her creative nonfiction has appeared in *There and Back* and *Buffalo*, the Sunday magazine of the *Buffalo News*.

Lorraine Elena Roses is Director of Latin American Studies and Professor of Spanish at Wellesley College, Wellesley, Massachusetts. The author of *Voices of the Storyteller: Cuba's Lino Novas Calvo*, she collaborated with Ruth Elizabeth Randolph on the award-winning book *Harlem Renaissance and Beyond: Literary Biographies of 100 Black Women Writers, 1900–1945* and *Harlem's Glory: Black Women Writing 1900–1950* (Harvard University Press, 1996).